The Bride of Christ Without Spot or Wrinkle

The Bride of Christ

of

Christ

Without Spot or Wrinkle

DR. PATRICIA VENEGAS

Table of Contents

Dedication

This book is dedicated to you, the body of Christ, His bride!

Also it is dedicated to my husband and children and their children and children's children till our Lord and Savior returns!

Acknowledgements

First and foremost I want to give glory, praise, and thanksgiving to our Lord and Savior for healing and restoring me. I would hate to think of where I would be today if it had not been for the Lord.

I want to especially thank my husband, Benjamin. Sweetheart, you are the wind beneath my wings and you have allowed me the privilege to grow and to be all God has called me to be. Without your love and support none of this would be possible.

Also, I want to acknowledge and thank my children, Pamela, Deborah, Thomas and Michelle. You have watched me grow to become the woman of God that I am today. You had to walk through this journey with me. I am forever grateful to the Lord that He has allowed me to be the mother of four amazing people.

Finally, I want to thank the editors, Dr Larry Keefauver, Russell Kent, David Truax and Reina Wendel. Thank you very much for your hard work and knowledge in assisting me with this book.

Acknowledgments

Introduction

———⁕❧⁃⟨◈⟩⁃☙⁕———

*G*od thought of you in a personal, saving relationship from the foundation of the world. Your personal salvation was not only well planned but demonstrates God's abiding faithfulness, as He prepares the consummation of His great plan for His Bride (the church). Spiritually speaking, the church is called, "The Bride of Christ". Up to now the bride of Christ is simply betrothed or engaged, much like Joseph was to Mary before the birth of Jesus (Matt. 1:18-20). The wedding day awaits. John saw a vision of the end of time, *Let us rejoice and be exceedingly glad, and let us give the glory unto Him: for the marriage of the Lamb is come, and His wife has made herself ready* (Revelation 19:7). The bride's splendid clothing was then described as the righteous acts of the saints (v. 8).

When Jesus comes again, He will come to present the church to Himself a glorious church, not having spot or wrinkle or any such thing; (Ephesians 5:27) [1] Ephesians 5 tells us,

Husbands, love your wives, even as Christ also loved the church, and gave himself for it; That he might sanctify and cleanse it with the washing of water by the word, That he might present it to himself a glorious church, not having spot, or wrinkle, or any such thing; but that it should be holy and without blemish. So ought men to love their wives as their own bodies. He that loveth his wife loveth himself. For no man ever yet hated his own flesh; but nourisheth and cherisheth it, even as the Lord the church: For we are members of his body, of his flesh, and of his bones. For this cause shall a man leave his father and mother, and shall be joined unto his wife, and they two shall be one flesh. **This is a great mystery: but I speak concerning Christ and the church.**

Nevertheless let every one of you in particular so love his wife even as himself; and the wife see that she reverence her husband. (Ephesians 5:25-33)

Preparing for the Bridegroom

What are we His bride doing to make ourselves ready for the "marriage supper of the Lamb"? (Revelation 19:7-9) Are we fully prepared for his arrival?

In Matthew 24:42-44, Jesus tells us to be alert and ready because we don't know the hour of His return. He also gives us the parable of the ten virgins to illustrate what it means to be ready and alert.

Then the kingdom of heaven shall be likened to ten virgins who took their lamps and went out to meet the bridegroom. Now five of them were wise, and five were foolish. Those who were foolish took their lamps and took no oil with them, but the wise took oil in their vessels with their lamps. But while the bridegroom was delayed, they all slumbered and slept.

And at midnight a cry was heard: "Behold, the bridegroom is coming; go out to meet him!" Then all those virgins arose and trimmed their lamps. And the foolish said to the wise, "Give us some of your oil, for our lamps are going out." But the wise answered, saying, "No, lest there should not be enough for us and you; but go rather to those who sell, and buy for yourselves." And while they went to buy, the bridegroom came, and those who were ready went in with him to the wedding; and the door was shut.

Afterward the other virgins came also, saying, "Lord, Lord, open to us!" But he answered and said, "Assuredly, I say to you, I do not know you."

Watch therefore, for you know neither the day nor the hour in which the Son of Man is coming (Matthew 25:1-13).

To understand the parable of the ten virgins one needs to understand the ancient Jewish wedding customs. The Jewish people are still practicing many of these customs today.

Jewish Wedding Traditions and the Gospel

The ancient Jewish wedding would begin with what is called the *shiddukhin* (a formal promise to marry at some future date). This was the arrangement made before the betrothal (engagement).

Then a contract was written up called a *ketubah*. This is the marriage contract detailing the conditions and provisions of the proposed marriage. Once both parties agreed to it, it was time for the engagement ceremony called the *erusin* (betrothal).

As the future bride and groom would prepare for the betrothal ceremony they would each take a ritual bath (immersion) separately in a mikvah. (*Mikvah* is also known as waters of purification. This is where Christian water baptism was originated.)

After the mikvah the young couple would meet under the huppah. The huppah was made from the groom's prayer shawl called a talit (fringes, Num.15:37-41). It is a structure supported by four poles. Symbolically the bride was coming under the groom's spiritual authority.

Then the groom would pay the father of the bride a bridal payment called a *mohar (Genesis 34:12, Exodus 22:16-17)*. Jesus paid the price for us. We read in 1 Corinthians 6:20, *For you were bought at a price; therefore glorify God in your body and in your spirit, which are God's.*

The groom would then pour a cup of wine and offer it to the bride. If she accepted the cup, it meant she agreed upon the conditions of the marriage. Matthew 26:27-29 reads, *And when He had taken a cup and given thanks, He gave it to them, saying, "'Drink from it, all of you; for this is My blood of the covenant, which is poured out for many for forgiveness of sins. But I say to you, "I will not drink of this fruit of the vine from now on until that day when I drink it new with you in My Father's kingdom."*

At this point, the couple was legally betrothed. They then made arrangements for the wedding. The groom would go away to prepare a place for the two of them to live. This was an addition to the groom's father's house. John 14:1-4 Jesus says, *Let not your heart be troubled; you believe in God, believe also in Me. In My Father's house are many mansions; if it were not so, I would have told you. I go to prepare a place for you.And if I go and prepare a place for you, I will come again and receive you to Myself; that where I am, there you may be also. And where I go you know, and the way you know.*

Only the father could release the son to receive his bride. Mark 13:32 reminds us, *But of that day or hour no one knows, not even the angels in heaven, nor the Son.* Acts 1:6-7 also speaks of God's timing, *Therefore, when they had come together, they asked Him, saying, "Lord, will You at this time restore the kingdom to Israel?" And He said to them, "It is not for you to know times or seasons which the Father has put in His own authority."* But before the groom left he would leave gifts for the bride-to-be. Jesus left us the gift of the Holy Spirit. *Peter said to them, "Repent, and each of you be baptized in the name of Jesus Christ for the forgiveness of your sins; and you will receive the gift of the Holy Spirit." (Acts 2:38)*

A year or so later the bride would be waiting eagerly for her groom. While the groom was away preparing a place for the two of them, the bride was preparing for the wedding by making her wedding garments. She would not know the exact hour that her groom was coming to get her; she and her bridesmaids had to be ready at all times to make sure that she was always prepared, day or night, for when her groom would come and sweep her off her feet. Traditionally the groom would come at night, **so the bride always made sure she had her lamp lit and lots of extra oil.**

The arrival of the groom would occur at an hour that neither he nor the bride would know. As the wedding day drew close, only the father could give the command for his son to get his bride.

As the groom approached the city where the bride lived, a horn (*shofar*) would sound alerting the bride that her groom was coming. The final step in the wedding process is called *nissuin*. The word comes from the Hebrew verb, *nasa* which means "to carry." A wedding procession would then carry the bride back to the home of the groom's parents. Then they would meet under the *huppah* again and exchange vows.

He would then take her away to their wedding chamber where they would stay for seven days. After the seven days, they would emerge together and participate in a gigantic feast with friends and family members. This was called the "marriage supper" and it would officially bring the wedding celebration to a close. Revelation 19:6-9 describes:

And I heard, as it were, the voice of a great multitude, as the sound of many waters and as the sound of mighty thunderings, saying, "Alleluia! For the Lord God Omnipotent reigns! Let us be glad and rejoice and give Him glory, for the marriage of the Lamb has come, and His wife has made herself ready." And to her it was granted to be arrayed in fine linen, clean and bright, for the fine linen is the righteous acts of the saints as we read, "Then he said to me, 'Write: Blessed are those who are called to the marriage supper of the Lamb!' And he said to me, 'These are the true sayings of God.'"

After all the celebrating, the married couple would depart to their new home that the groom had prepared for them. Just as the bride and groom would emerge and return to their new home, so too will we return with our Messiah to our new home that He has prepared for us. [2] Revelation 21:1-10 continues:

Now I saw a new heaven and a new earth, for the first heaven and the first earth had passed away. Also there was no more sea. Then I, John, saw the holy city, New Jerusalem, coming down out of heaven from God, prepared as a bride adorned for her husband. And I heard a loud voice from heaven saying, 'Behold, the tabernacle of God is with men, and He will dwell with them, and they shall be His people. God Himself will be with them and be their God. And God will wipe away every tear from their eyes; there shall be no more death, nor sorrow, nor crying. There shall be no more pain, for the former things have passed away." Then He who sat on the throne said, "Behold, I make all things new." And He said to me, "Write, for these words are true and faithful." And He said to me, "It is done! I am the Alpha and the Omega, the Beginning and the End. I will give of the fountain of the water of life freely to him who thirsts. He who overcomes shall inherit all things, and I will be his God and he shall be My son. But the cowardly, unbelieving, abominable, murderers, sexually immoral, sorcerers, idolaters, and all liars shall have their part in the lake which burns with fire and brimstone, which is the second death." Then one of the seven angels who had the seven bowls filled with the seven last plagues came to me and talked with me, saying, "Come, I will show you the bride, the Lamb's wife." And he carried me away in the Spirit to a great and high mountain, and showed me the great city, the holy Jerusalem, descending out of heaven from God.

Defining Our Words

I love to study the Hebrew words and their meanings. Through this study I have found that the name for LORD is Yahweh, for God is Elohim, for the Holy Spirit is Ruach Hakodesh and for Jesus is Yeshua.

LORD (*YHWH*): The Tetragrammaton from Greek: τετραγράμματον, meaning "consisting of four letters." In the Hebrew Bible, God reveals His name to Israel as *YHWH* over 6,700 times. When vowels are added to *YHWH* the name reads *Yahweh*.

God (*Elohim*): "*Elohim*" denotes what linguists call a **plural of majesty, honor, or fullness**. That is, he is GOD in the fullest sense of the word. He is "GOD of gods" or literally, "*ELOHEI* of *Elohim*" (Deuteronomy 10:17; Psalm 136:2).

Holy Spirit (*Ruach Hakodesh*): The *Ruach Hakodesh* is the comforter and spirit of *Yahweh*. He is very significant in that we need the *Ruach Hakodesh* to be able to walk before *Yahweh* at all times; the *Ruach* will lead us in all truth. He is a very precious part of Yahweh which has been given to those who are in Yeshua.

In this book I will be referring to Jesus by His Hebrew name, *Yeshua*. It means "*Yahweh* [the LORD (*Yahweh*)] is Salvation." Salvation is full restoration according to *Strong's Concordance* (Hebrew: 3468 salvation: deliverance, rescue, salvation, safety, and welfare). Salvation is all-inclusive: spiritual, emotional, moral, social, relational, and ultimately life eternal, by the power of the blood of *Yeshua* at Calvary. *Yeshua's* blood has bought and paid for our salvation, but the continued work of becoming God's (*Elohim*) holy people is a life-long journey of presenting ourselves to God (*Elohim*), and to the Holy Spirit (*Ruach Hakodesh*) for transformation. Our loving and gracious God (*Elohim*) desires for His people to be whole in all aspects.

Preparing to Read and Study with Prayer

Before you begin to read, pray this prayer of preparation .

Father, I want to be without spot or wrinkle or any such thing. I want to be one of the virgins who has oil in her lamp and who is ready for my bridegroom. Please prepare me for your soon return.

Father, your word says, "Hear, you deaf; and look, you blind, that you may see. Who is blind but My servant, or deaf as My messenger whom I send? Who is blind as he who is perfect, and blind as the Lord's servant? Seeing many things, but you do not observe; Opening the ears, but he does not hear."

Father, I do not want to be your servant that has eyes but can't see or ears and can't hear. Give me spiritual eyes to see and open my deaf ears that I can hear your voice clearly in these last days; Guide me by your eye and not a bit in my mouth.

Give me the spirit of wisdom and revelation in the knowledge of You.

In Yeshua's name, Amen!

Chapter 1

My Testimony

—◦⟨∘⟩◦—

And they overcame him by the blood of the Lamb and
by the word of their testimony, *and they did not*
love their lives to the death.
(Revelation 12:11)

I was born on November 14, 1953 in Long Beach, California. I am
the youngest of five children. When my father, Howard Moore,
met and married my mother, Bessie, she had four children from a previous
marriage. My mother had self-aborted five previous pregnancies and was
told by her doctors she could not carry any more children. However, my
father had always wanted children. Doctors told him that he was sterile
due to a chemical exposure while serving in the Army in World War ll.
Despite what my mother and father were told, I was born against all odds.
My mother bled throughout the entire pregnancy.

When I was a couple of months old, my parents moved our family to
Amarillo, Texas, where my mother had been born and raised. They rented
a house approximately three miles from her parents, Johnny and Winnie
Whisenant.

My grandmother, Winnie, was a loving and caring mother and
grandmother. She had given birth to six children. Sadly, when in her
twenties, she had three-month-old twins that died for the reason that she
was unable to produce breast milk due to lack of food. She told me that
when they died her heart hurt so much she couldn't bear to be in the
house alone. Because of her deep grief, she asked my grandfather if she

1

could go to the cotton fields to pick cotton just to get out of the house. He agreed. While she was in the cotton fields, she tried to pick cotton, but her heart was so overwhelmed with anguish she could not get her babies off her mind; she could not bear another moment. She fell to her knees, clutching her apron towards her eyes, sobbing so hard she felt as though her heart would come out of her chest. The pain was excruciating. She said in that very moment an angel appeared to her out of nowhere and brought comfort and peace to her; peace that passes all understanding. God (*Elohim*) healed her grieving, broken heart. That day she became a born again, spirit filled woman of God (*Elohim*). From then on she served the Lord (*Yahweh*) wholeheartedly.

Most Sundays she would take my siblings and me to church. On the way to church, I remember her turning around to the back seat, where I was sitting, reaching over the big blue and white backrest of the front seat of the car, spitting on her flowered embroidered handkerchief, and wiping the dirt off of my face. I hated those spit baths. However, it is because of her that I fell in love with God (*Elohim*). After church we would go to her house to eat. As soon as we would walk in her front door the aroma of her chicken dinner would be in the air. I will never forget those dinners, they were delicious. My parents, my uncle, and the children would crowd around her kitchen table to enjoy her home-cooked meals. I look back and wonder how we all fit in that small kitchen. It was so tiny. The house itself could not have been more than 800 square feet if that. My grandfather had built it when they first got married. Originally it had an outhouse and there was no drain in the kitchen sink. You had to throw the dishwater out the back door. Later he added a bathroom. Each of the three rooms were very small: a kitchen, a bedroom, and a living room where my grandparents slept. Years later, as an adult, I went back and could not believe how small that house was. The house was no more than six feet tall.

One sunny, cool, breezy Texas Sunday morning, when I was three years old, my four siblings and I decided to attend a little church across the alley behind my house instead of attending my grandmother's church where we were regulars. We were bickering for forty-five minutes about who was and who was not going to attend. Most of them did not want to go. When my mother had enough, she angrily said, "None of you are going to church." I remember all morning thinking to myself, "I AM going to church no matter what." After she said no one was going, I thought, "Oh YES I AM!" I snuck out of the house in my pajamas, with my hair a mess, and my cowboy boots on, and I went to church. I remember sitting in that Sunday school class as the other children stared at me. I am sure I must have been a sight. I didn't care. I just loved being there. I don't even know if I went to the right children's class, but I listened to every word that teacher said. My heart was so full of love for God (*Elohim*). When I returned home, my father was in the driveway with the police. My parents had called them out of worry, because I was missing. After asking where I had been, the police could not believe I was at church the whole time. Since everyone was so relieved to see that I was okay, I was not punished.

We moved from Amarillo, Texas to Lawndale, California three days before my sixth birthday. When my parents moved us back to California, I continued to hold God (*Elohim*) close to my heart by always talking to him. There was a little church on the corner not far from my new home which, I only attended occasionally, since I had no one to take me.

Growing up in California

Without my grandmother nearby and her godly influence, my family became more dysfunctional. My parent's alcoholism along with my mother's "legal" drug addiction- her doctors would prescribe any medication she wanted- made my childhood a living nightmare. The house was dirty and cockroach-infested. I did not want anyone to see my home. If I ever had someone pick me up for anything, I would ask them to pick me up blocks away from my house, so they would never know where or how I lived. I felt a lot of shame due to my living conditions.

In my home there was domestic violence, as well as mental, physical and sexual abuse. I remember one night my sister snuck out of the house after my father had gone to sleep. For whatever reason, he woke up and waited in the kitchen with the lights turned off, waiting for her to come home. I still remember sitting in the living room watching TV, looking into the dark kitchen, hearing his heavy breathing and smoker's cough, seeing the tip of his cigarette light up with every puff. When my sister came home, she tried to sneak in as quietly as possible. She asked me in a whispered voice, "Is dad awake?" About that time he came flying out of the kitchen. Like a mad man, he pushed her up against the front door, and started screaming and cursing at her and began punching her in the face with his closed fist. I sat frozen with fear. I watched this unfold in front of my eyes and I could do nothing to help. I will never forget the sound of flesh on flesh as his fist made impact on her face.

Another traumatizing thing that happened in my home included my parent's excessive drinking. After they would come home from the bar or the horse races, they would beat each other up. Though both of my parents were committing adultery and my father was heavy into pornography, my father would accuse my mother of trying to sleep with other men. They would scream and cuss at each other. These fights would go on for hours. Many times I would be awakened in the middle of the night by their cussing and screaming knockout fights. Not knowing what to do, I would lie there in my dark bedroom, fear gripping and overwhelming me.

Other times there were drunken parties that would nearly always end in fistfights. I remember in one fight someone was knocked through the large pane living room window. Due to all of these events the police were called regularly.

Because of my parent's drinking and gambling, there was no money for bills, groceries, or rent. This forced us to have to move out of the houses we were renting. Some years we would move two or three times. I would have to change schools each time. It was hard to fit in at these new schools. Trying to fit in, at the age of nine, I started smoking cigarettes. By the time I was eighteen, I was smoking three packs of cigarettes a day.

I ditched school a lot because of the rejection I felt due to the poverty that came along with the dysfunction and alcoholism. I would go to school wearing old worn clothes, passed down from my sisters. They were dirty because of my mother's lack of hygienic skills. I don't even remember taking baths or having my hair combed. One dark cold winter night, when I was seven, I was outside on my back porch playing with the little girl that lived in the house behind us. She took her shoes and socks off. Her feet were so clean and white! I could not help compare them to my black and dirty feet.

Since some of my shoes were too big for my feet, I would put toilet paper in the toes to make them fit. I remember one pair had a hole in the sole, yet my parents said that I could wear them a little longer because the hole wasn't that bad. So, I started tearing at that hole to make it bigger, just so I could get a new pair. On a couple of occasions I was sent home from school, because I had no socks to wear.

One school morning, when I was in the second grade, I remember feeling so cold, it felt like the cold went all the way to my bones. I didn't have a sweater or coat to wear and my clothes were too thin for the season. I was shivering in line with my teeth chattering, waiting to go into class. The girl in front of me offered me her sweater and I accepted it. The sweater was warm, clean, and soft. I just couldn't get over how good it smelled and how good it felt.

Growing up I did not go to school much, but when I did, I was always hungry. I could not concentrate. I remember one time I was so hungry that I stole someone's lunch and went in the bathroom to eat it during recess. That lunch tasted so good. Right before lunchtime, the teacher wanted to know who took the child's lunch. She was not going to release the class until somebody confessed. I was not about to confess. I felt so embarrassed.

My parents never attended any of my school functions. In third grade, I played the lead character in a child's play called *Rumpelstiltskin Is My Name.* I watched the audience all morning, hoping my parents would show up. I was disheartened when they did not come. However, my oldest sister, Judy, did show up. She was more mother-like to me then my actual mother.

When I graduated from eighth grade, I was not going to attend my graduation, because I did not have a dress and my parents were not going to be there. However, my friend and her mother insisted that I go. They were amazing. My friend lent me one of her dresses, a pair of shoes, and fixed my hair. I am grateful they were so caring.

Throughout my childhood my nickname was dumb-dumb. By the time I was eighteen years old, I believed myself to be stupid. I genuinely believed I could not learn anything. There was no encouragement to learn academics or to focus in school. Growing up in a dysfunctional home, all I learned was how to survive. I believe now that children raised in dysfunctional homes, as I was, have a really hard time learning, because they are in survival mode. When your parents' fighting keeps you up all night, or when you witness the abuse of your siblings, when you are abused, and when you go to school hungry, it is very hard to concentrate on learning.

During my childhood, I had been molested multiple times. I used to say it was like I had a sign on my forehead that read, "Come and molest me." One can imagine the damage that does to a child. Now I know that it was because of the lack of supervision from my parents and because I found it difficult to say *no.* I had no voice and no boundaries.

I think the molester that affected me the most was my brother-in-law. When I was twelve years old he began having sexual relations with me. This went on for about six months. I kept it hidden because I felt I was to blame. I felt somehow it was my fault. I felt so much shame and guilt. Since it was my brother-in-law, I was afraid that if my parents and sister found out they would be very angry with me. One day when I was at a girlfriend's house,

5

we were talking in her bedroom and I confided in her about what was happening. When I left, she told her mother right away, and her mother told my parents. When my brother-in-law found out that they knew, he told me to say we just held hands, and nothing else happened. My father questioned me. I told him the truth. He let it drop and did nothing about it. My sister wanted me to go to her house to talk about it. I was very frightened of her. I did not know what she would do to me, so I refused. Years later we talked. She reassured me that she was not mad at me, that she did not want to hurt me and that it was not my fault.

All of this led to my high-risk lifestyle with no boundaries, I became pregnant at thirteen years of age. I met my daughter's father, Bruce, not long after the molestation stopped. He was sixteen and I was thirteen. Shortly after we started seeing one another we were involved sexually. This, too, was more like molestation. I really did not know how to say no. I was very naive and uneducated about my reproductive system. I thought I was pregnant, when I was not. We decided to run away with another young couple that lived next door to me. We were going to move to another state with this couple. Since they lived next door to me the plan was for Bruce and me to go to Los Angeles, get a hotel room, and wait a couple of days for them to join us. This way my parents would not suspect that they had anything to do with my disappearance. While we were waiting those couple of days, I got pregnant.

We stayed in downtown Los Angeles, California, near Pershing Square. We had been hanging out at Pershing Square when we met some people that Bruce seemed to befriend. One day, while we were there, a woman was preaching. As I listened to her, I could feel a tug in my heart. I wanted to hear everything she had to say. She asked if there was anyone that wanted to receive Christ as their Lord and Savior. I raised my hand and went forward. I did not care that there was a crowd around me and that no one else responded. She had me close my eyes and bow my head as she prayed with me. I already had a love for God, because of my grandmother, but I don't think I had asked him to be my Lord and Savior. I surrendered my life to him that day. I remember asking the Lord to come into my heart and for his will to be done in my life. I felt so good after that prayer. It felt like a weight had been lifted off of me.

Unfortunately, Bruce did not feel the same. He was upset. To him, I had embarrassed him in front of his new friends. About a half hour after I prayed that prayer, everything changed. We found out that our friends had changed their minds at the last minute. They no longer would be joining us. They decided they did not want to move out of state. It seemed all of our plans had fallen apart, and now Bruce was mad and upset. He just wanted to take me home.

After he took me home, we called his parents. They came and got him and forbade us to see each other any longer. They were sure my child was not his. They wanted no part of the pregnancy. My mom was very angry with me. My parents decided I should go and live with my Aunt and Uncle for awhile. This was a very difficult time for me. I was home schooled and separated from my friends.

Looking back this probably saved my life. The friends I had hung out with got into heroine. Since I did not know how to say no, I might have followed after them. One of the girls died of an overdose. This was the era of the hippie movement. After I gave birth to my daughter and went back to school, I could not believe that the "good kids" were now drug addicts. The classrooms were crazy. I don't know how the teachers were able to teach. I remember talking to a girl in class whose speech was slurred and it looked like she wanted to sleep. I couldn't understand what was wrong with her. I was so alarmed I thought there must be something really wrong. As I tried to get the teacher's attention, one student said, "Be quiet, she is stoned." I didn't know what that meant. They had to call an emergency response team, who took the girl away in an ambulance. Kids were walking around "stoned" everywhere. It became a common thing for them to be carried out on stretchers.

I ended up going to a continuation school which is for the "troubled kids." To my surprise the "troubled kids" had it together more than the kids in regular school. They were there to learn, get their work done, and get out.

Even though in those days having a baby at thirteen was unheard of, I wanted to keep my baby. I am so thankful I did. I love her so very much. When Pamela was born on October 1, 1967, she weighed 7 lbs. 6 oz., and was 19 inches long. She had blond hair and looked like a doll. Because of her, I now have four wonderful grandchildren and four great-grandchildren. I cannot help wonder how many people are not here because of abortion. Not only is the person who was aborted not here, but the whole bloodline of that person is missing due to the abortion.

Due to my mother's emotional hurt and pain, she would self-medicate with prescription drugs. She lied to get them. She would go to doctors and tell them she was in pain. However, they could not find anything wrong, so they would perform *exploratory surgery.* She would go to the hospital for two to three weeks at a time. (In those days they would keep you there that long) Looking back now, I realize that the time in the hospital, for her, was a vacation from us kids. We would be left at home to fend for ourselves. My father had a full-time job. When he was not at work or at the hospital with my mother, he was at the bar drinking.

Growing up, I knew there was a hell, because I was living in it. I had tried killing myself a couple of times, because I did not want to live any longer. My first attempt was when I was nine years old and my mother was in the hospital. All us kids were left alone. We were fighting, as usual. My sister Beverly, who is two years older then I, would not leave me alone. She followed me from room to room trying to provoke me to fight her. As my sister continued to aggravate me, I had a random thought, "*I wonder if you dream when you're dead.*" So I went to the bathroom, opened up the medicine cabinet, and took out a bottle of my mother's pills. I swallowed all fifteen of them, one by one.

As I walked to my bedroom to lie on my bed, my sister trailed behind and continued her remarks until she finally said, "I wish you were dead!" I replied back to her, "So do I! Get out of here and leave me alone so I can die!" She ran out of the room and told Judy what I said. Judy came into my room right away to ask if what Beverly told her had any truth to it. She asked if I had taken anything. While she was interrogating me and I was denying it, the phone rang. Strangely enough, it was my father checking up on us before he went to the bar. Judy told my father what I said to Beverly. My father asked to speak to me, so I went to the phone.

He asked, "Have you taken anything?" I said, "No." While I was speaking to my father I could feel myself getting sleepy. I could not wait to go lie down and close my eyes. As soon as I got off the phone I went straight to bed and fell right to sleep.

My father decided to come right home instead of going to the bar. That was so unlike him. When he got home he asked Judy where I was. She told him I was in bed. He went to my room and found me lying on my bed, lifeless. He could not wake me up. I did not respond to him calling my name and shaking me as hard as he could. Panic swept over him as he called the police. When the police arrived, they could not wake me up either. They took me to the hospital and pumped my stomach. I spent two days there before I woke up.

My second attempt was when I was fifteen years old. I had started to waitress at fourteen to support my baby and parents. My father had been injured on a job and had lost his little finger, so he was not working. Neither was my mother. It was so hard to support all of us. At fifteen I moved out of my parents' house. I thought it would be easier to live on my own. I was wrong. I felt really lost. I started dating a lot. I was looking for love. Growing up I had always felt lonely. Now that loneliness intensified.

I had just broken up with a boyfriend, and I felt rejected again. It felt like my life was over. I felt so alone. I ended up taking a whole bottle of pills. As I lay on the floor waiting to fall asleep, I was thinking how all the hurt and loneliness was going to end. When the sun streamed through the slit in the curtains and woke me up the next morning, all I could think was, "No God, no. Why won't you let me die?" Anger towards him flooded my body. I was thinking he was mean for not letting me die and for making me stay in this hell.

My First Marriage

I met my first husband, Bill when I was sixteen and working at an Armenian restaurant in Torrance, California. He came in one night for dinner with his daughter Lisa. She was three years old, a year older than my daughter Pamela. She had dark straight hair and a sweet smile. She was so cute and bouncy. As I was taking Bill's order, Lisa told him she had to go to the bathroom. I could tell he felt awkward taking her into the men's room, so I volunteered to take her. After I brought her back to the table he seemed to flirt with me. When they were ready to leave, he asked me out and we began dating. Within a month I moved in with him.

Bill was eighteen years older than I. He was divorced. His ex-wife was a nurse who was more interested in her career than being a mother to Lisa. It wasn't long before Lisa moved in with us and I became her primary caregiver. Her mother would only see her occasionally.

Bill and I were married when I turned eighteen. Not long after we got married, we started attending a church. However, we continued living in our sinful lifestyle of watching pornography, smoking pot, and drinking alcohol.

Somehow through all of that, the Lord still moved. I remember being invited to attend several Full Gospel Business Men's meetings. These meetings were great. I heard personal testimonies of how God (*Elohim*) changed people's lives. These stories really touched me. At one of these meetings they spoke about the baptism of the Holy Spirit (*Ruach Hakodesh*).

I really wanted to be baptized with the Holy Spirit and receive my prayer language, which is speaking in tongues. Not long after this meeting, I was in prayer asking for this gift. The Holy Spirit came on me very strong and

I started praying in my prayer language. I now look back and see, although God did not change me all at once, He had begun a great work in me.

There are two works of the Holy Spirit: one is to lead us to accept Christ and be baptized; the second is to fill us so we can truly live the Christian life and do the works of God.

Yeshua said all who believe would do even greater works than He. When a believer receives the baptism of the Holy Spirit, they are empowered to do the same works as Christ because Christ has filled him (Mark 16:17). Before experiencing this Spirit infilling, God is with the believer because He called him to accept Christ and led him to be baptized. However, he will not have the fullness of the Spirit's power within him until he receives the baptism of the Holy Spirit. That is why Yeshua told the disciples to wait for the outpouring baptism of the Spirit on the day of Pentecost before they began their ministry for Him.

Soon after, I decided I wanted to quit smoking. In order to quit, I tried oil painting. I thought it would take my mind off of the cigarettes as well as help me to not gain weight. I remember the first time I touched a brush to a canvas. One morning I went to see a friend with whom I often had coffee. When we would get together, I would often complain about my marriage and discuss how upset I was becoming. This particular morning my friend had her set of oil paints and a canvas set up on her kitchen table.

She suggested I sit down and try my hand at painting something. The painting I did was dreadful, still painting made me feel really good emotionally. I had never felt like that before. For that short time, all of my hurt, sadness and anger towards my husband disappeared. It was as though I was somewhere else. It felt like going on a vacation and leaving behind all of the stress back home. When I sat down to paint, I lit a cigarette. I put the cigarette down in the ashtray and it burned out.

After that morning, I enrolled in painting classes at the local community center. The teacher had me paint a white water pitcher, round vase, and an orange. I was so proud of that painting. When I brought it home my husband laughed at it. He told me to give it to my mother for only she could appreciate it. I did, and she did. She had it hanging on her kitchen wall until the day she died. I thought to myself, "I do not care if I have to put every one of my paintings under the bed. Painting makes me feel so good emotionally." The feeling of accomplishment I received from learning something was amazing. I thought I could never accomplish anything because my parents and family always called me, dumb-dumb. The Lord (*Yahweh*) used these classes to build my self-esteem. Through learning how to oil paint, God

(*Elohim*) showed me that if you have the right teacher and the right material, with some effort, you can learn almost anything. Through the painting I was able to quit smoking, and I did not gain weight.

After four years of marriage, I found myself very unhappy and did not know why. Bill had been staying out at night until early morning from the very beginning of our marriage. He became very distant and was not available emotionally. (As I look back, I think he was into more perverted sexual sin then I could imagine.) One day he dropped me off at the same friend's house that had me paint. He was supposed to pick me up in an hour. He said he had to do something with the car. Hours went by and I needed to pick up my children from school. I borrowed my friend's car to get the children. On my way back to her house, I saw him with a woman in our car. I called home, only to find out he had been there with the woman. I questioned him concerning his whereabouts and about the woman. He gave some lame excuse saying he just picked her up because she needed a ride somewhere. He had to stop by the house because he forgot something. Today, as I think back she probably was a prostitute.

As a blended family, there were issues regarding how unfair he was to my daughter Pamela. His daughter Lisa would do things in front of him just to put him and me at odds.

He was an electrical engineer with Hughes Aircraft and made a good living. However, he was really cheap when it came to Pamela and me. At one point I needed a winter coat and had asked to buy one. He refused. Later that same week we were at the mall. He was looking at a leather sport coat that was very expensive. He asked me how it looked on him as he admired himself in the mirror. I said it looked fine. Then I asked, "If you can afford that, why can't I get a winter coat?" When we left the store, he slugged me in the arm for making him look bad in front of the saleslady.

When I asked for a trial separation, he went to an attorney, had legal separation papers drawn up and had me sign them. He said if we get a divorce those papers would turn into divorce papers. I didn't know anything about divorce, but throughout our marriage he told me how bad his ex-wife was and how much money she stole from him. All I could think of was I never wanted to be like that.

I thought if I got a divorce, it would solve all of my problems. Then I would find some sort of happiness. After my divorce, instead of happiness, I found loneliness to a degree that I had never experienced even though growing up I had always felt alone. I felt like I was dangling in outer space-like I was going to fall any minute. I was sent into an emotional tailspin.

11

I was such an emotional wreck, I was no good for anyone. I moved out of the house and into a small apartment. This was such a hard time for Pamela and Lisa. Pamela had her own bedroom when I was with Bill, now she had to sleep on the couch. Lisa wanted to come and live with me. To her I was her mommy. She did not understand why I left her behind. Instead of pressing into God (*Elohim*), I defaulted back to what I knew. I went back to being a waitress at a restaurant that served alcohol. It did not take long before I went back to drinking heavily. I had gone from being a mommy of two little girls, who took them to church, to a mommy who stayed out drinking and bringing strange men home.

Now along with being a waitress, I was selling my oil paintings at art shows. During one of the art shows I met Dave, an NCIS agent. He kept asking me to marry him. I finally said, "Yes." Pamela and I moved in with him. We moved to Long Beach, California. Once again, I moved Pamela to a new school. After Dave and I were engaged he had to go away for some training. While he was gone, Paul, the restaurant manager started making advances toward me. One night I was counting my tips and he sent me over a drink. It was one of those sweet drinks. Before I knew it, I had too much to drink that I could not drive home. So Paul drove me home. That was the beginning of a relationship, even though he was married. Pamela and I were still living with Dave. I was such an emotional mess, I was not there for Pamela at all. I cannot even imagine what it was like for her through all of this. I now see how Satan uses our hurt and pain to hurt others.

Two weeks before I was to be married to Dave, Paul left his wife and wanted me to move in with him. I broke off the engagement to Dave. Pamela and I moved to San Pedro with Paul. Once again, Pamela had to change schools. I was so far away from God (*Elohim*). This was such a self-destructive relationship. It was based on lust, seduction and perversion.

After three months of living with Paul, he went to get more of his things from the house that he shared with his wife. While he was gone I felt the Lord tugging at my heart, calling me back to him. I knelt beside my bed and started praying. I had been very far away. I was in such a dark place spiritually. Not only was I drinking, but I was smoking pot again.

At that moment, I surrendered my heart back to God. I told the Lord if he wanted to take Paul out of my life and restore his marriage, I was willing. I wanted what God wanted for me. Paul came to our apartment three hours later and told me he was going back home to his wife. Within two days my life was turned upside down. We had bought furniture together and he took all of it with him and left me my share of the money. My apartment was empty, apart from a record player and a record. The record was *For Those Tears I Died*. I don't know how it got there. I never bought it. I was brokenhearted. I lay on the floor crying for hours as I listened to that song over and over again. These are the lyrics of that song (Words and music by Russ and Marsha Stevens, 1972).

For Those Tears I Died (lyrics)

You said You'd come and share all my sorrows,
You said You'd be there for all my tomorrows;
I came so close to sending You away,
But just like You promised You came there to stay;
I just had to pray!

And Jesus said, "Come to the water, stand by My side,
I know you are thirsty, you won't be denied;
I felt ev'ry teardrop when in darkness you cried,
And I strove to remind you that for those tears I died."
Your goodness so great I can't understand,
And, dear Lord I know that all this was planned;
I know You're here now, and always will be,
Your love loosed my chains and in You I'm free;
But Jesus, why me?

And Jesus said, "Come to the water, stand by My side,
I know you are thirsty, you won't be denied;
I felt ev'ry teardrop when in darkness you cried,
And I strove to remind you that for those tears I died."
Jesus, I give You my heart and my soul,
I know that without God I'd never be whole;
Savior, You opened all the right doors,
And I thank You and praise You from earth's humble shores;
Take me, I'm Yours.

And Jesus said, "Come to the water, stand by My side,
I know you are thirsty, you won't be denied;
I felt ev'ry teardrop when in darkness you cried,
And I strove to remind you that for those tears I died."

Even though I prayed that the Lord would take Paul out of my life, it was still very hard emotionally. It amazes me to this day how much God loves us even when we are broken and hurting as a result of our own highrisk, self-sabotaging lifestyle. The Lord spoke so clearly to my heart saying, "No matter who leaves you, I will never leave you nor forsake you." Our Father has seen where we have come from, and He knows where we are going. He knows the plans he has for us, plans to bless us and not to harm us. There is a destiny for us and He is trying to get us to fulfill it.

My Second Marriage

After Paul went back to his wife, Pamela and I moved back to Torrance, California. (I think Pamela must have gone to three schools in that year alone.) We had lived in Torrance when I was married to Bill. It seemed like I kept going back to what was familiar. I felt lost, again dangling in midair. I started dating again and praying for a husband. I thought if I could just find the "perfect" man to marry me, I would be happy. I was out one night with friends in a nightclub. A man named Tom, whom I had served at the restaurant and had known for a year as a customer, sent me over a drink, I went over and joined him. I found out that he too was a *born again Christian*. I spent that night with him. We talked all night long. He told me his father recently passed away, and his mother had passed a year earlier. His sister Susie was a Christian singer who traveled to different churches to sing.

This was around the time when the Hippie movement was becoming the Jesus movement. Christian coffee houses with Christian music sprang up everywhere. Susie was part of this movement. She had been on tour in Kansas and was staying in a farmhouse. One morning, the kitchen sink became clogged. The owner of the farmhouse owned a propane truck. He decided that he could unplug the sink by hooking up the hose from his truck to the sink and blowing out the stoppage. There was a water heater in the kitchen; the propane ignited, and there was a huge explosion.

Susie was walking into the kitchen right when it exploded. She yelled, "Jesus," which caused her to exhale instead of inhale. This saved her lungs, however she was burned so badly that her bra melted into her skin. Tom had to fly to Kansas in a rented plane and bring her home. This happened right after his father's passing He brought Susie home, and took her to a San Pedro hospital. There were many Christians praying for her. Tom told me it was like watching time-lapse photography. God performed a miracle. God had healed her.

When he shared all of this with me I thought, "This man is the answer to my prayers. We will go to church together and I will be a stay-at-home Christian mom." Everything would be wonderful. I knew if I could just marry a Godly man, he would be able to put my life in order. This man was going to be my savior, and give me everything I needed emotionally, so I thought Soon I would know that no man, except the Son of God, can be anyone's savior.

Tom and I dated for two and a half weeks before we got married. I thought, *God had answered my prayers, why wait?* Because we got married so fast, our wedding day happened to fall on Tom's poker night. Tom played poker once a week. As we were setting the date of our wedding, he told me, "I am not going to miss my poker night."

So after the wedding I went with him, in my wedding dress, and sat in the living room, by myself, while he played poker with his friends. I remember thinking what a wonderful person I was. Not every new bride would allow her groom to go to his weekly poker game on her wedding night without complaining. All of his friends could not believe how wonderful I was to not ask him to miss his game. For our honeymoon, he had a bass fishing tournament planned and told me I could come along if I wanted.

Tom had two daughters, Kelly and Stephanie, from his first marriage. We decided that God had put us together, so we wanted to have a child together right away. Within twenty-five months we had two more children, a daughter, Deborah and a son, Thomas Jr. When Deborah was born she looked like a china doll. She had porcelain white skin with dark hair. She was very beautiful. When I would hold her and look at her, my heart would do somersaults. However, it was very hard on Pamela. Not only did she have to change schools again, she now had two more stepsisters and a new baby sister. I had to work, so I had very little time with Pamela. My oldest stepdaughter was very mean to her. One day she curled up in my arms and said she wished we could go back to being just the two of us. I said, "We wouldn't have Deborah, your baby sister." She said, "That would be fine." Pamela was hurting so much.

I remember the time I got pregnant with Thomas Jr. I had just lost the baby weight from being pregnant with Deborah. I thought I would never get pregnant again. Then I heard the voice of the Lord, and He asked me if I would get pregnant again and I said, "Yes Lord." I was pregnant before

15

I knew it. I believe my son was meant to be here. Ever since I had Pamela, I had wanted a son. However, the circumstances at the time seemed to scream that this is the worst time ever to get pregnant again. This would make five children and our finances were horrible.

After I got pregnant, I remember laying on my bed and thinking "What have I done?" Not only was it hard financially, but I was having problems in my marriage. Tom was always gone. I thought, "Lord this man is not going to meet my needs. I do not feel he loves or cares about the kids and me." I wanted love very badly. That's when I heard the Lord say, "No man can meet your needs, but I can. I am going to give you love, and it is going to be so much that you can give it away freely, without ever needing man to give it back to you." Then He likened it to a millionaire that had so much money he could write hundred dollar checks to people all day and never worry if they could pay it back. Then I felt him pour that love into my heart.

When Thomas Jr. was born he was almost nine pounds and twenty-three inches long. He looked like a worried old man. Most babies are born with a glaze look in their eyes, as though they can't quite see yet, but not him. He was looking the Doctor up and down, seemingly asking, "Who are you and what just happened to me?"

My husband Tom was never around, and I felt single inside of this marriage. He had so much hurt and pain, from his divorce and the passing of his parents that he was unable to be there emotionally for all of us. When he was not working or fishing he would be depressed, spending most of the time in bed.

When Tom's father passed away he left Tom and his sister a business, a paint store, in San Pedro, California. His sister did not work at the paint store at all. Tom was not happy working there. He felt as though he wanted more freedom and more money. Tom loved to bass fish. If he was not going away for the weekend to fish, he would often go fishing all night out of San Pedro harbor. Afterwards, he would want to sleep all day. When I saw that he was not opening up the Paint Store until one or two o'clock in the afternoon, I started going in and running the store. San Pedro is a small fishing town. The people there were faithful customers because of Tom's father.

Tom had a family friend, Richard, who wanted his own business. So Tom refinanced our house that we had bought in Rancho Palos Verdes and took the money to start a business with Richard. In Tom's mind he thought Richard would run the business and make him rich. Then he would not have to work and he could go fishing more often. Our house payment went from a thousand to four thousand dollars a month, in 1980. Financially it was very difficult. I was working three jobs to make ends meet, and I was also running the paint store.

In February 1980, I found myself in my living room, on my knees with my face buried in the couch, crying out to God. I was determined I was not going to leave there until I received the answers I desperately needed. I was so disillusioned with life. I was twenty-six years old. I had already been through one marriage that ended in divorce and was in my second marriage. It was not working either. Now, I had six children, two babies sixteen months apart, and four teenagers. One of these was Lisa, from my first husband Bill. He passed away not long after our divorce. Lisa wanted to come and live with us. I couldn't take on any more responsibility. I was there to help her as much as I could, but I could not bring her into our home.

It seems silly to say this now, but I did not know what I was doing wrong. It seemed that the choices I was making for my life were all the wrong ones. That day I gave up. I was bankrupt in every area of my life: emotionally, physically, financially, and relationally. All I could do was cry out to God. I just wanted to be happy. What was I doing wrong? I was attending church (without my husband), and I was praying. I thought I was doing all the right things. However, they were not working.

The Lord met me that day in my living room, in such a powerful way. It was as though the whole room filled up with an overwhelming presence, a warm heaviness, however, light at the same time. There was such sweetness. I felt very warm, as though warm oil had been poured over my whole body. My breathing increased; it became very heavy. The Lord started speaking to me, not in an audible voice, rather from within, to my heart and mind.

When the Lord started speaking to me that day, He said, "Your emotions need to be healed. You need to go back to your past, emotionally, to have the hurt healed." He explained to me that I was like a computer that had been programmed. I could only make decisions based on what I knew. If you do not have a different perspective, you will not know how to do things differently.

What did He mean, *"Go back?"* I was confused, because I was attending a church and they taught that, *Therefore if any man be in Christ, he is a new creature: old things are passed away; behold, all things are become new* (II Corinthians 5:17). I was told I did not need to look back on my past. When they told me this, I was very relieved.

I did not want to remember my past. Besides, hadn't I dealt with it? I thought I had, but all I had done was bury it. There was so much emotional

17

hurt. When a memory would surface I would push it down as fast as I could, hoping no one knew what I was thinking. There was so much shame, guilt and regret, not only as a result of what had been done to me, but because of the things I had done. I had been looking for love in all the wrong places.

I remember one morning, right after my eighteenth birthday, being in my kitchen and it dawned on me, I had survived. I made it through my childhood. I literally held on to my kitchen counter with both hands, saying to myself out loud, "I made it. I am eighteen, and I never want to or have to go back there." I was so relieved. I never wanted to remember all the emotional pain of rejection, molestation, fear, shame, guilt, etc

Now, I was in my living room on my knees, in the presence of the Lord. He was telling me He needed me to go back to be healed. I did not want any memories to come to mind. I did not want the emotional pain associated with them. I had worked hard to forget what I had been through.

The Holy Spirit led me to open my Bible. As I did, I turned to the book of Isaiah 61, *The Spirit of the Lord GOD is upon me, because the LORD has anointed me to preach good tidings to the poor; He has sent me to heal the brokenhearted, to proclaim liberty to the captives, and the opening of the prison to those who are bound.* The Lord said through that same inner voice, He was going to heal me and bind up my broken heart.

Chapter 2

A Vision of Two Brides

---

*Husbands, love your wives, just as Christ also loved the
church and gave Himself for her, that He might
sanctify and cleanse her with the washing
of water by the word, that **He might present her to
Himself a glorious church, not having spot or wrinkle
or any such thing, but that she should
be holy and without blemish.***
(Ephesians 5:25-27 emphasis added)

When the Lord said He was going to heal me emotionally, He
gave me a vision of two brides. The first one was filthy. Her
hair was a mess, greasy and all out of place. Her make-up was smeared
with mascara streaks down her checks from her tears. The dress she was
wearing was tattered and ripped, with dirt and black oil stains all over it.
The second bride was so beautiful, it is so hard to describe her. She was
radiant. Her dress was glowing white, and she had every hair in place with
her makeup perfectly applied.

He said, "The first bride is what my church looks like today. The second
one is what I am coming back for, a bride *without spot or wrinkle.* I
am sending you to the church, not a denomination, but the believers in
My Son, the whole body, to bind up the broken heart, to set the captive
free. My bride is hurting on the inside and I am going to heal, restore and
cleanse her.

You can see when someone has a variety of illnesses or has broken bones. However, you cannot always see when a person is broken emotionally. Many times they do not want people to know what they have experienced or where they have come from. Just like you, they too have learned to bury their pain and pretend there is nothing wrong. They wear masks to hide the truth, pride, vulnerability, fear, anger, sadness, depression, shame, guilt and regret, along with the emotional pain. Many are too proud to let people know who they really are. Many are afraid that if others really know who they are they would not love them."

Then He said, "When you get into heart issues, sometimes demons will surface." I thought, "What do you mean demons?" The first thing that came to my mind was the movie, The Exorcist. The Exorcist is a 1973 American supernatural horror film, directed by William Friedkin, and adapted by William Peter Blatty from his 1971 novel of the same name. The book, inspired by the 1949 exorcism case of Roland Doe, deals with the demonic possession of a twelve-year-old girl and her mother's desperate attempts to win back her child through an exorcism conducted by two priests. This movie really scared me. I remember being overwhelmed with the feeling of fear. I did not want any part of any exorcism. For the next six months the LORD (*Yahweh*) would talk to me about demons. I did not want to hear anything about them. I told the Lord, "I will do the emotional healing part, whatever that is, but I want nothing to do with demons." [3]

The anointing came upon me.

I had changed churches and I was now attending Bethany Christian Fellowship, a small Foursquare church in San Pedro, California. My pastors' were Augie and Debbie Herrera. They were great pastors. I was attending regularly and teaching the two-year-olds. One Sunday, Pastor Debbie's mother was a guest speaker. Her message that day was about Calvary and what *Yeshua* did for us on the cross. It was powerful. At the end of the service she said that God wanted to give us an extra blessing. If anyone wanted this blessing they were to come forward. She said, "Take off your shoes you're on Holy ground. Lift your hands and start praising God." So I took off my shoes and lifted up my hands. As I did, everything in me was praising HIM.

As we were praising God, the power of the Holy Spirit came upon me strongly. My body felt as though it was two inches tall, and the Holy Spirit in me felt as big as the block the church sat on. I was crying uncontrollably, my body was shaking violently. It felt stronger than an earthquake that registered "10" on the Richter scale. I was shaking so hard, that as I tried to wipe away my tears, I was slapping myself in the face. I am not sure how long this lasted. It could have been as long as an hour, but no less than twenty minutes. This was more powerful and stronger than the baptism of the Holy Spirit (*Ruach Hakodesh*) I had already received.

I then started to prophesy. This is what the Lord began to say through me: "We are moving into the last days. Right now there is still a middle road between good and evil, light and dark. There is a time coming that the middle road will no longer be here. You will either be for God or you will be for Satan. By not being for God you are on Satan's side. Some believers are holding on to sin. They think they will be able to get out of it. They still have time before the end. Darkness is getting very dark. If they cannot quit sin now while it is still light, they will not be able to be set free. The very thing that Satan is using to hold them in bondage now, will be the very thing he will use to destroy them and take them to Hell with him."

When the power of the Holy Spirit lifted, I could not believe what had just happened. To say I was astonished and overwhelmed by what just happened to me is an understatement. I do not even have words to describe or try to share with you what this felt like. I remember walking out of the church building, saying to God, "YOU ARE SO BIG AND SO POWERFUL." The Lord said, "That was nothing. It was not even a drop in a bucket. You could not contain ALL OF MY POWER." He brought the subject of demons up again and said, "Most people are not aware that there is a force in the spiritual realm. Some people see objects moving, or have a sensation that they are being watched. Some feel that something or someone is in the room with them, but they cannot see anything, etc. Many people think these are ghosts, but they are not. They are demons. Satan and demons have power. You are to understand they have power. However, I AM ALL POWER." My life has never been the same from that day forward. I know the word of God is all truth and that God is very real.

This was different than being baptized in the Holy Spirit (*Ruach Hakodesh*). The LORD (*Yahweh*) has shown me that He anointed me that day for the call and mandate that is on my life: to cleanse the bride and make her ready for the return and second coming of *Yeshua*.

The Lord started an emotional healing process in me. He gave me, *My brethren, count it all joy when you fall into various trials, knowing that the testing of your faith produces patience. But let patience*

21

have its perfect work, that you may be perfect and complete, lacking nothing. If any of you lacks wisdom, let him ask of God, who gives to all liberally and without reproach, and it will be given to him. But let him ask in faith, with no doubting, for he who doubts is like a wave of the sea driven and tossed by the wind. For let not that man supposes that he will receive anything from the Lord; he is a double-minded man, unstable in all His ways (James 1:2-8).

When the Lord gave me this scripture I thought He must have made a mistake. How could I count everything I was going through as joy? Did He not know how bad things really were in my life?

My marriage was worse than ever. When Tom married me he never gave me his heart. Throughout the marriage I would tell him, "I love you" and he would say, "I know you are going to leave me like everybody else. You will stab me in the back like everyone has." He had so much hurt and pain from his past marriage due to his ex-wife cheating on him with his best friend, and because of the death of his parents, he had put so many walls up around his heart that I could not get in.

The business that Tom had started with Richard went bankrupt. We could no longer keep the house. It kept going into foreclosure. We had to sell it along with the paint store, because of all the financial problems we faced. Tom was more unavailable now than ever before. If he was not in bed for days, depressed, he was gone. Meanwhile, I was waitressing, cutting hair, selling Jafra and my oil paintings to support the household. When Tom worked he would give me very little money, if any, at all.

On New Year's Day that year, I went to the grocery store, not necessarily to buy groceries, but to get out of the house. I walked around the store, not thinking about food, but more or less in a daze, feeling numb, thinking, "I cannot do this anymore." I could not see me going through another year in this marriage without change. There was no working on the marriage because Tom was not there emotionally.

When I got home from the store, I went in the front door and straight to the kitchen to put the groceries away. I looked into the living room and I saw Tom sitting on the couch. I went over, sat down, and the words just starting pouring out of my mouth. It seemed like I could not stop them. Before I knew it, I asked him for a divorce. I had not really thought about how this would play out. I just knew in my heart I could not keep doing what we were doing.

He was very upset! I remember him crying. It was hard for me to feel anything at that moment. I didn't have any compassion for him whatsoever, which was unusual for me.

After he moved out it was harder for me than I expected. I had never wanted a divorce. I felt like a failure, because this was my second one. One of the reasons I stayed for as long as I did was because I am a Christian and I thought, "No matter what, I have to make my marriage work."

I kept thinking, "You are a Christian, you cannot get a divorce." So, when my family and I were going to celebrate my son's birthday at Chucky Cheese, I invited Tom to join us. As soon as he arrived he started drinking. He continued throughout the party. By the time we left he was really drunk. He followed me back to our townhouse and I invited him in, thinking I have to really try to make my marriage work.

It was way past the children's bedtime, so I took them upstairs to their rooms and put them to bed. I prayed with them as I tucked them in. I left Tom downstairs with my sister Judy and her boyfriend Ron. While I was upstairs, I heard a loud noise. I went downstairs to investigate. Tom was sitting at the kitchen table and had gone into a rage, banging on the table with his fist. He looked like a wild man. His eyes were glazed over. I had never seen him like this before. I could feel my heart pounding, and I could hear my pulse in my ears. I became terrified. As panic struck me, I felt I had to leave immediately.

I picked up my purse and car keys and started running for the front door as fast as I could. I opened the front door and I made it out to the patio area. Tom came up behind me and started attacking me. He lunged at me, pushing me up against the block wall. I hit the wall hard with my left shoulder. He put his hands around my throat, and as he tightened his grip, I thought I would pass out.

Judy was living with me at the time, and she went to the phone right away and called 9-1-1. I was scared and trembling. My heart was beating so fast. I do not know how I got the strength and managed to get out of that chokehold, but I did. I was able to make it to my car, even though he was right behind me and kept pushing me. When I got into my car, I was trembling so hard it was hard to get my keys into the ignition. I didn't think to lock the door. Just as I started the car, Tom swung the door open. He reached in between the steering wheel and my body, turned off the ignition, and took my keys. He threw them over the chain-link fence and into the townhouse's swimming pool.

I felt trapped. Fearing for my life, something in me snapped. I came out of that car like a crazy person. I started hitting him and pushing him away from me towards the front of the car. He tripped over the concrete

23

parking bumper. He fell backwards and landed on his back and I started jumping up and down on his chest.

When the deputies finally arrived, I was so relieved. I felt safe. It seemed like it had been hours, but in reality it was only a few minutes. He ran up to the deputies and told them I attacked him and it was unprovoked. I could not believe the personality change. He was like two different people, from raging and attacking me, to becoming extremely calm as if nothing had happened. As I told my side of the story to them, one deputy looked at my neck with his flashlight, saw the choke marks and said, "Someone has been choking her."

They said they would arrest both of us if we didn't stop fighting. They asked if I had some place to go. I told them I did. I spent the night at a friend's house. Every time I thought I would try to make the marriage work, Tom became abusive.

One weekend I went away with some friends. When I returned home, I found Tom had come in and taken all the furniture. I had hidden money between my mattresses, and I had forgotten to take it to the bank before I left for the weekend. I could not believe how insensitive he was, not only towards me, but also towards the children. He didn't seem to care if the kids had a refrigerator or a table to eat on. After nine and a half years of marriage, it ended.

As I was praying one day about this marriage, the Lord showed me that He had not put me in this marriage, I had put myself in it. There was such insecurity in me, feeling that no one would want me. I learned that people that rush into marriage are afraid that the person they are going to marry will find out who they really are and will not want to marry them. Many times we are more in love with the idea of being in love.

A Vision of Two Flowerbeds

The Lord gave me a vision of two flowerbeds. He said there were two gardeners. The first one knew everything about gardening. He turned the soil, took out the rocks and fertilized it. He knew just what plants to plant, and how much sun and water they needed. The flowerbed was beautiful. It flourished. The second gardener knew nothing about flowerbeds. He did not turn the soil, or take out the rocks, nor fertilize it. He knew nothing about plants and just threw some seed on the ground. One plant barely made it. The gardener would walk by that plant and see it barely holding on, with little green left in the stem of its wilting flower. He would give it just enough water to survive.

The Lord said these two flowerbeds represent the way we grew up. How we were raised affects how our needs were met. Just like those gardeners, some parents know how to raise children and know what they need in order to flourish; however, others know nothing and just have children.

We are putting together a puzzle of life, and depending on what flowerbed we were raised in, determines how many puzzle pieces we get. At the time he showed this to me, I was attending a church where my pastor's parents were not perfect but emotionally healthy. They met their children's basic needs: housing, food, clothing, and emotional support. His dad worked, while his mom stayed at home. His parents went on date nights, and went to church. His dad even coached their little league games. When my pastor turned eighteen, he knew what he wanted to do in life. He went on to college and married his wife in his early twenties. They are still married today, some forty years later. The Lord said my pastor had been born in the first flowerbed. The Lord said he received ninety-seven percent of his puzzle pieces. However, I had been born in the last one. Barely surviving, I got three percent of mine.

Unknowing, we go through life looking for the rest of our puzzle pieces. When we get into relationships we expect the other person to give us the rest of our pieces. This becomes the problem because neither person wants to give away what little they have. Our needs, which were not met growing up, are the ones we are trying to fill. I had been trying to get my puzzle pieces.

People who get their needs met by the time they turn eighteen are thinking of what they want to be and do in life. When people are raised in dysfunction and do not get their needs met, they think only of surviving and getting their needs met that they did not receive as a child.

We do this by picking what is familiar to us. (In emotionally healthy people this is a good thing.) I had picked what was familiar to me. I did this in several ways. Tom was a *Christian* and he drank. My thinking at the time was that this is great, because he could go to church with me and get along with my family at the same time, because they all drink.

I had learned to take care of my mother instead of her taking care of me. She was always depressed and suicidal. When I met Tom, that night in the club, he was depressed. Throughout our marriage he was depressed and if I ever tried to deal with real issues he would become suicidal. I felt if I loved him enough, I could make him happy and he would not be depressed anymore. The Lord told me I was not God, and I was not someone else's happiness. I was doing the same song and dance I did with my mother, and it did not work with her either.

When I was a little girl, I would fall asleep with my head on my father's hairy chest. He would wrap his hairy arms around me. I remember those were times I felt safe and loved. I would not date anyone that did not have hairy arms and chest, no matter how well they treated me. Tom had hairy arms and a hairy chest. This reminded me of my father.

My brother, Rick, had a protruding Adams-apple. He fished and was never around. I loved my brother, however, I never really connected with him, because he was always gone. Tom also had an Adams-apple, fished, and was always gone.

All of these things, on a subconscious level, reminded me of my mother, father and brother. I was trying to get the needs met that my family members did not meet in my childhood.

I look back and see that Tom married what was familiar to him also. Everyone who met me and who knew Tom's mother would say, "You are so much like his mother." He would never remember my birthday, but when it was Mother's Day he would shower me with gifts. He would tell me to tell him what his mother used to tell him, "Everything is going to be okay."

God started showing me that, as I was trying to get my needs met, I had also been rescuing Tom.

I truly thought this was the good part of me. I had so much pride thinking I could work three jobs and take care of my family. All the while I would be crying out to God telling him how tired I was. At the same time, I would protect Tom from any consequences of his actions because of His depression. I didn't think he could emotionally handle people being angry with him, so I would take care of everything and everyone for him.

The thought of letting go of this part of me terrified me. I gave up drinking, drugs, sleeping around, cussing, gossiping, lying, etc. However, when the Lord wanted to deal with this part of my character it was the hardest part to give up. When God started to deliver me from my dysfunction of rescuing, I said to him, "If I give up the good part of me, who will I be? I will be empty, nothing." God said, "Exactly." That is what He wanted, so He could fill me up with Him.

Proverbs 22:6, *Train up a child in the way he should go, and when he is old he will not depart from it.* This is a wonderful scripture if you were raised in a Godly home. This was given to a people that were to raise their children to follow God and his loving instructions. But in our society we have gotten so far away from the way God wants us to live and raise our children.

When we are going through trials and tribulations, the Lord is working in our lives to mature us, and to restore His original plan for our lives. James 1:4 says, *But let patience have its perfect work, that you may be perfect and complete, lacking nothing.* In Greek the word *perfect* means; endurance, constancy, stead-fastness, and perseverance. When we go through these trials it causes us to mature and grow up in the things of God.

Romans 8:26-30 reads, *Likewise the Spirit also helps in our weaknesses. For we do not know what we should pray for as we ought, but the Spirit Himself makes intercession for us with groaning's which cannot be uttered. Now He who searches the hearts knows what the mind of the Spirit is, because He makes intercession for the saints according to the will of God (Elohim).*

Rescuing is "not wanting someone else to hurt because you know what that feels like." By rescuing others we think it will make ourselves feel good and protect others from feeling bad. We find ourselves rescuing other people because we wanted somebody to come rescue the little boy or the little girl that we were. And though we are physically grown, many of us have not been healed in our emotions. Our emotional hurt, insecurities, memories, trauma, and fears that we went through as children rule our adult life and many times we are not aware of what we are doing.

Our behaviors and actions towards others allow us to not accept that we were once child victims because we now have the power to fix things. Ultimately we derive a false sense of being in control, which provides us a sense of empowerment. But that feeling does not last long because we find ourselves involved in relationships with friends, family members and lovers who are lifetime victims or dependents who have no idea how to be there for us.

Rescuing others is an unconscious addiction that springs from our need to feel valued and to prevent others from walking out of our life. It's even more difficult to accept that after all the time and energy spent trying to fix things for others that we can't expect anything back from them. Many of these relationships will end because the other person is needy and does not have the ability to care for him or herself and they have nothing to offer to anyone else.

Rescuers are attracted to victims and dependents. The end result is we wind up becoming serial victims. We are trying to fix someone else. This keeps us busy so we don't look at ourselves. The Bible tells us to take the board out of our own eye before we can get the speck out of someone else's. [4]

For whom He foreknew, He also predestined to be conformed to the image of His Son, that He might be the firstborn among many brethren. Moreover whom He predestined, these He also called;

whom He called, these He also justified; and whom He justified, and these He also glorified.

In the beginning of going through my divorce with Tom, the Lord gave me the following vision...

I was walking in a desolate, dry, rocky desert. The rocks were sharp, and I was barefoot. My feet were bleeding from being cut up on the sharp rocks. The Lord (*Yahweh*) said to lean on him and let him carry me. He would help me through. Off in the distance I could see beautiful green, lush rolling hills. The Lord said when I get through this desert place I would be in that land that is green and rich, no longer dry and rocky. (Where I live now, I have lush green hills all around.)

I have two beautiful children, two stepdaughters, and five wonderful grandchildren from that marriage.

Chapter 3

The Bridegroom, Bride and Boaz

─•ᐭᕲᕱᕲᕲᕶ•─

I went to a Bible study one night, with a friend, after I started my divorce. The teacher was teaching on the book of Ruth. The setting for the Book of Ruth begins in the pagan region of Moab, a region northeast of the Dead Sea, then moves to Bethlehem. This true account takes place during the miserable days of failure and rebellion of the Israelites, called the period of the Judges. A famine forces Elimelech and his wife, Naomi, from their Israelite home to the region of Moab. Elimelech dies and Naomi is left with her two sons, who soon marry two Moabite girls, Orpah and Ruth. Later both of the sons die, and Naomi is left alone with Orpah and Ruth in a strange land. Orpah returns to her parents, but Ruth determines to stay with Naomi as they journey to Bethlehem. This story of love and devotion tells of Ruth's eventual marriage to a wealthy man named Boaz, by whom she bears a son, Obed, who becomes the grandfather of King David and the ancestor of *Yeshua*. Obedience brings Ruth into the privileged lineage of Christ.

A major theme of the Book of Ruth is that of the kinsman-redeemer. Boaz, a relative of Ruth on her husband's side, acted upon his duty as outlined in the Mosaic Law to redeem an impoverished relative from their circumstances (Leviticus 25:47-49). Christ, who redeems us, the spiritually impoverished, from the slavery of sin, repeats this scenario. Our heavenly Father sent His own Son to the cross so that we might become children of God (*Elohim*) and brothers and sisters of Christ. By being our Redeemer, He makes us His kinsmen. After hearing this great story, not only did I feel like the Lord was my kinsman-redeemer, I thought, "Lord, I need a Boaz."

I met Benjamin at the restaurant where I worked after Tom and I had to sell the paint store. Benjamin was a detective with the Los Angeles County Sheriff's department. He was asked to become a detective the same time I started working at the restaurant. He would come in and eat lunch two or three times a week with his coworkers. He had been coming in for two years when he overheard me talking to a coworker about me cutting the owner's mother's hair. (This is one of many ways the Lord had blessed me to bring in extra income.) He told me his sergeant had been on him to get a haircut. He said he had been trying to get one for some time, but for one reason or another it never worked out. Since I could tell he really needed his haircut, I gave him my phone number and address, so he could come to my townhouse after work.

After the haircut I invited him to McDonald's with the kids and me to have dinner. While eating he had asked me, "What is your dream in life?" I told him, "My dream has turned into a nightmare. All I wanted was to be a Godly wife and mom and have a Godly home." None of that seemed possible at the time. I remember thinking I will never get married again. I will never give my heart to anyone ever again. It was too painful. I believed marriage was a joke God played on people. You would lust after one another then you would live in hell after you got married.

I never had a strong role model for a healthy marriage, but God started showing me healthy marriages. There was a Christian couple that had been coming into the restaurant. They had been married for fifteen years. As I observed the two of them together, I couldn't believe what a great relationship they had. They were best friends. This actually gave me hope for marriage.

In April 1987, Benjamin and I started dating. We had a great courtship. Through it we became best friends. Throughout my life I had always felt lonely. I no longer felt that way. Benjamin truly courted me. We were married on the anniversary of our first date, April 17, 1988.

I was of the opinion that if it was your second or third marriage, as was my case, you should not wear white. So I bought a purple dress for our wedding. One morning I was in prayer, and I heard that inner voice of the Lord again. He told me to take the purple dress back. I was to buy a white dress. Then the Lord said, "This marriage represents Me and My bride. My bride is dirty from the world and she is hurting. However, I am washing and restoring her with My word and blood, to present her to

Myself a bride without spot or wrinkle or any such thing. You are clean because of that blood." Wow!

The Lord has truly blessed me with my Boaz and has blessed our marriage. We have been married twenty-seven years and we have one daughter from our union, Michelle.

Benjamin had never been married before, and when he married me he automatically became a father and grandfather. He had hoped for children of his own; however, after my son, Thomas was born, I decided to have a tubal ligation. When Benjamin found this out, he still chose, out of his love for me, to marry me.

After our marriage I found out about a medical procedure called In Vitro Fertilization (IVF). IVF, in simple terms, is a process where the woman is put on fertility hormones, and they retrieve an egg/eggs from her ovaries and take the sperm from the father to fertilize the egg/eggs. Then they put them in the woman's uterus.

This is not an easy or inexpensive process. Your hormones and emotions are all over the place. When we first started this process I prayed about it and I felt the Lord say that I was going to get pregnant. The doctors said there was a one in four chance that I would get pregnant. So, on my first day in the doctor's office, I looked around that small room. I saw three other women sitting there, two across and one next to me. I sat there thinking, "Praise God! There are four women in here, and I am the one that is going to get pregnant."

The process was not as easy as I thought it was going to be. I had to start giving myself shots for thirty days. Then, for two weeks, I had to drive in traffic for an hour to down town Los Angeles at five o'clock in the morning. When the doctors determined that it was time to retrieve the eggs. I went in as an outpatient, and they gave me light anesthesia while they retrieved the mature eggs. Two days later I returned so they could implant them into my uterus. Then we had to wait to take a pregnancy test. I was so excited that I had heard from the Lord, I knew I was going to be the one in four to get pregnant. We got the news I was pregnant. We were so happy. God was so good.

Then I started bleeding, I called the doctor and he said that was normal. However, the bleeding got worse, and I started to hemorrhage. I called the doctor back and he told me to go to the emergency room. When we arrived at the hospital, Benjamin let me off at the emergency room front doors, so I could get medical aid as soon as possible. While he went to park the car, I walked to the front desk. I could feel myself getting weaker and weaker. I just wanted to go to sleep. I had lost a lot of blood. The doctors did an emergency D&C on me. I had miscarried. I was devastated. How could it have been? I had heard from the Lord. What happened? I went into a tailspin emotionally. When I returned home, I did not want to feel the emotional pain. So I got busy, really busy. I started wallpapering my bedroom. I must have looked like a Tasmanian devil. I kept thinking, "Just get busy, really busy, so you don't have to feel."

I was in emotional darkness. I thought I was losing it. Satan started beating me up emotionally. Thoughts were running through my mind like, "Yea and you tell people you hear from God ...You don't hear from God, etc."

In this frenzy, the Lord started showing me that I was getting really busy in order to avoid pain.

Avoidance & numbing: It can be just too upsetting to re-live your experience over and over again. So you distract yourself. You keep your mind busy by losing yourself in a hobby, working very hard, watching TV, etc. You avoid places and people that remind you of the trauma, and try not to talk about it. You may deal with the pain of your feelings by trying to feel nothing at all – by becoming emotionally numb. You communicate less with other people who then find it hard to live or work with you.

I had not realized that my hard work, and working three or four jobs, were also a way of avoiding or numbing my feelings. Again, I thought my hard work was a good thing. Now the Lord was showing me it was a way of escape. He wanted me to feel the grief of the loss and to let Him heal me.

The procedure to get pregnant took a toll on us both emotionally as well as financially. After trying several more times, over a two and half-year period, to no avail, we were exhausted and ready to give up. Benjamin was leaving for work one morning, and we were asking ourselves if we should try again or just call it quits. We decided to pray about it. As Benjamin left for work, he said, "You pray and I will pray on my way to work."

After he left for work, I started praying. Again, I felt that sweet presence of the Holy Spirit come upon me. It was like the time in my living room, when the Lord said He was going to heal me.

The Lord told me that this pregnancy was like Hannah in the Bible. Hanna was the mother of Samuel. She too could not get pregnant. The Lord said He laid it on her heart to conceive. After she conceived and gave birth to Samuel she gave him to the Lord.

The Lord said that He gave me the desire in my heart to conceive, because I did not previously want any more children. Deborah and

Thomas were now at the age where it was easier to take care of them. I did not want to start over with an infant.

The Lord said this child was meant to be here for this child's generation. At the time, the pastor of the church we were attending was forty years old. The Lord said when this child is forty, my pastor would be eighty. There would be an anointing on this child.

After the Lord spoke this to me, Benjamin and I tried again. Throughout this process many eggs had been fertilized, but none took. On our final try, the doctors retrieved two eggs. The doctors said out of those two eggs one was not mature enough to use. However, when we returned for them to implant the fertilized egg, the doctor said the mature egg ended up with two sperms fertilizing it. They said they weren't going to use the mature egg. Instead, they would use the immature egg that was fertilized. After 2 ½ yrs. of trying, with that immature egg, I conceived Michelle.

When I was six months pregnant I started bleeding. I thought I was going to lose the pregnancy. We went to the emergency room. They did an ultrasound. The baby was fine. The technician asked what name we had picked out. I said Matthew, because it means a gift from God. I thought the baby would be a boy. She said we might think of naming the baby Michelle However, she said she could not tell me the gender of the baby.

Michelle Victoria (her name means who is like God victorious) was born June 15, 1992, a month earlier than her due date.

The Lord said that it had to be that sperm and that egg. Through this process I realized that none of us are a mistake. Even the timing of our conception and the timing of our birth is perfectly planned by our maker.

For You formed my inward parts; You covered me in my mother's womb. I will praise You, for I am fearfully and wonderfully made; Marvelous are Your works, and that my soul knows very well. My frame was not hidden from You, when I was made in secret, and skillfully wrought in the lowest parts of the earth. Your eyes saw my substance, being yet unformed. And in Your book they all were written, the days fashioned for me, when as yet there were none of them. How precious also are Your thoughts to me, O God (Elohim)! How great is the sum of them! (Psalm 139:13-17)

I have such compassion for women who cannot conceive. It is emotionally painful when you want children and you cannot get pregnant.

Our Blended Family

When I married Benjamin, Pamela was already married and had two children. I still had Deborah and Thomas at home. Blending a family was not easy. Benjamin was a very strong disciplinarian. He had been in the army, and was now in law enforcement. I was the opposite. I was raised in a home where, as long as you did not get brought home in a police car you could pretty much do anything you wanted. I would be gone for hours without any accountability. No one checked my homework or made sure I went to school.

I remember right after we married he came home from work and asked if the kids had done their homework. I said, "Yes."

He asked, "Did you check it?"

I said, "No."

"How do you know they did it?", he asked.

"Because they told me they did", I replied.

He called the kids out of their rooms and asked if they had done their homework. They told him they had. I thought, "See they did it." He asked to see their homework. They started making excuses why they had not done it. I could not believe they lied to me. From then on, he would check their work.

Deborah had a hard time with math. Every day, after a hard day at work, Benjamin would come home and sit down with her for one or two hours and help her with math. All the while she would be in tears. At the time, I could not understand why he would be so mean to my daughter. Now as I look back, it was a sacrifice for him to come home and help her.

Since Tom never paid child support, Benjamin sacrificed for my children and me. He worked overtime, so I could stay home with the children. He paid for them to be in a private, Christian school. Then he moved us to a new area that had great schools. This move added to his commute. When we bought a new van, he started driving the car that had everything breaking down on it, including the air-conditioning. He would drive between one and a half to two hours, in heavy Los Angeles traffic, in the middle of the summer, with no air-conditioning, so the kids and I could have the new van and be comfortable. At the time I could not understand why he was so upset when the kids would leave trash in the van. I thought that he was very unfair and that I was being spiritually attacked.

Benjamin was a very good provider. He put braces on Thomas' teeth and bought both Thomas and Deborah contact lenses instead of glasses, so they would not be embarrassed at school. There were times he needed a pair of new shoes because he had a hole in the sole; however, he wouldn't buy a pair so the kids could have their needs met.

I know that he loved us. However, there was such hardness in him. I did not understand it at the time. Now I believe a lot of the hardness came from Post-traumatic Stress Disorder due to the Vietnam war. He was drafted when he was eighteen years old. I cannot even imagine all that he went through at a young age. It must have been such a culture shock having been raised in a close, loving, caring family, only to be sent to serve your country in war time. Then your country, that you went to fight for, rejects you when you come home. No "welcome home hero", no "thank you" for just going to hell and back, because your government sent you there. (I think we as a country owe these vets a big apology.)

I know that Thomas and Deborah were hurt emotionally because of his hardness. I used to tell him, *it is not what you say; it is how you say it.* He was right in what he would tell us to do: *clean your room, eat at the table, wear shoes outside, do your homework, etc.* However, when he would correct us, it was with harshness and anger. In those days it seemed he was always angry. I know the Lord has healed a lot of his hurt. He has softened up. By the time Michelle was being raised, and the others had moved out, he was much softer. But, she never felt that he was soft or warm. She did not feel he approved of her. Even though he loves all of his children and grandchildren very much, they have never seen his heart the way I have.

I remember one time crying out to God and telling Him how hard my husband was on me. The Lord told me I was a bent tree, and He had put a steel rod next to me to straighten me up. He is more interested in our character than our comfort.

One weekend, Benjamin and I went to a marriage retreat. On one of the breaks from the sessions, we had time to go to our room and take a nap. As Benjamin was dozing off, he said, "I really love you, but I never knew how hard it was going to be to be married." After he went to sleep, I started praying. In my prayer, I prayed about the "irritants" in our marriage.

The Lord told me about the oyster and how it makes a pearl.

"A natural pearl begins its life inside an oyster's shell when an intruder, such as a grain of sand or bit of floating food, slips in between one of the two shells of the oyster, a type of mollusk, and the protective layer that covers the mollusk's organs, called the mantle.

In order to protect itself from irritation, the oyster will quickly begin covering the uninvited visitor with layers of nacre — the mineral substance that fashions the mollusk's shells. Layer upon layer of nacre, also known as mother-of-pearl, coat the grain of sand until the iridescent gem is formed. It's interesting that cultured pearls are made in the same way. The only difference is, instead of accidental circumstances, a pearl farmer embeds a grain of sand into the mollusk." [5]

Then the Lord said, "You are working on a pearl necklace and you are going to use all of these pearls of wisdom to help someone else."

Through all of these "irritants" I truly learned a lot. Benjamin and I have been "sandpapered," as we have grown emotionally and spiritually through our life together.

Benjamin is now retired and in ministry with me fulltime. Our children have grown up. We look back and think, "While we were going through it all, it seemed like a lifetime." Now it seems like a blink of an eye. Deborah followed in Benjamin's footsteps and became a deputy sheriff. She is married and has a wonderful son Jordan. Thomas is a commercial artist with his own business. He is married and has a beautiful daughter Lydia. Michelle wants to go into law enforcement. Presently she is an EMT. Pamela is married and is a real estate agent. She has four wonderful children and four adorable grandchildren. Due to all that the Lord has taught me about marriage, I have developed a teaching called, "Boot Camp for Marriage."

Chapter 4

The Gift of Counsel in the Bride of Christ

—❧⟨◉⟩❧—

For unto us a Child is born, unto us a Son is given; and the
government will be upon His shoulder. And His name
*will be called Wonderful **Counselor**, Mighty God,*
Everlasting Father, Prince of Peace.
(Isaiah 9:6)

*S*oon after Benjamin and I were married the gift of counsel by the Holy Spirit was released on my life greater than before. When the Lord gave me the vision in my living room that day, he told me he was going to first heal me and then send me to the whole body of Christ, to heal his people. This is exactly what started happening. People started seeking me out to minister to them emotionally and to get Godly counsel. The scripture he gave me that day was no longer words on paper. They were now living words. *The Spirit of the Lord God is upon me, because the Lord has anointed me to preach good tidings to the poor; He has sent me to heal the brokenhearted, to proclaim liberty to the captives, and the opening of the prison to those who are bound* (Isaiah 61:1). Our Father has heard the cry of His people, seen their tears, and He desires to bind up their broken hearts.

Many of us are going through life with emotional pain. Many times I would answer my phone, and I would hear a muffled broken voice on the other end. Sobbing, the person would be trying to get the words out, saying, "This might sound crazy but God keeps telling me to call you, I keep fighting it, but I just had to call you." After they would share their heart with me, I would start praying. The Holy Spirit would reveal to me what the true problem was.

I have had the privilege to see hundreds of people blessed by the power of the Holy Spirit as He would, and still continues to heal their emotional hurt.

What Is Deliverance? Deliverance is being set free from spiritual bondages and barriers that hold us back from walking in the victory that *Yeshua* won on the cross for us at Calvary. It is the driving out of evil spirits by the authority of *Yeshua*. Despite what many people think, deliverance is not about the demons. It is about being set free in *Yeshua*'s name. When deliverance is ministered properly, *Yeshua* is glorified and our lives are changed for the better.

After five years of counseling and praying for people to have their hearts healed, the Lord said we were going to move into setting people free through deliverance.

Within days of him telling me this, the very next person I prayed for manifested. It was at a women's conference I attended through my church for the weekend. At lunchtime I ran into a friend and she invited me to sit at her table. She said she was so glad that I was there, because she wanted me to meet her niece.

She introduced me to this young woman and had me sit next to her. I turned and started talking to her. Within minutes tears welled up in her eyes and soon the tears turned to uncontrollable sobs. I decided it would be better to find somewhere more private for her to share with me what was going on in her life. When we moved to a private room, she started pouring her heart out to me. She did not love her husband or her five children even though he was an amazing husband and her children were very good. She confessed she had never been able to love or receive love her whole life. She felt it was unfair to her husband to stay married to him even though he really loved her. She wanted to feel his love and love him back, but she was unable to.

Listening to how painful this was for her, my heart was overwhelmed with compassion. I sensed that the Lord wanted me to pray for her heart to be healed so her heart would be able to love her family. As soon as I started praying for her, a demon surfaced. At this time, I was under the belief that Christians could not have demons. However, her voice changed, her face contorted, and the demon started screaming at me to shut up. It said it wasn't going to let her heart go. The Holy Spirit had me tell the demon to shut up. It could not talk to me, in the name of Jesus. As I spoke this, her lips pressed together really tight and her head shook violently back and forth, as if she was saying "no." The demon could not speak any longer. This was my first encounter with a demon manifesting.

After the weekend, I ministered more to her and found there was a lot of rejection and abandonment in her life. In another of our sessions, when I began to pray for her, a demon manifested. She slumped out of the chair, and slithered to the floor while the demon was growling. I was commanding it to leave, however, it would not leave.

I started praying for the Lord to show me how to pray for her. He gave me a vision of her as a baby in a crib, crying hysterically for hours for mommy. But mommy never came. She was so young at the time of this rejection and abandonment she had neither memory nor words to express what had happened to her.

The Lord had me sit on the floor with her, hold her in my arms, rock her, sing Jesus Loves Me and pray for healing of that rejection in her life when she was a little baby. When I did, the demon, which had put walls up around her heart, lost its power over that emotional pain of rejection, which had caused her from receiving love as well as giving love.

The Lord told me many people have no memory of what happened to them before two or three years of age. However, from the time they are conceived and between two or three years of age, what they experience can throw them off balance for the rest of their lives. Many have no idea why they do or act in certain ways.

For a season, in every Christian I prayed for, demons manifested.

We read, *Yeshua called the twelve together and gave them power and authority over all demons and to cure diseases, and he sent them out to proclaim the kingdom of God (Elohim) and to heal (Luke 9:1-2). ...after this the Lord appointed seventy-two others and sent them on ahead of him, two by two, into every town and place where he himself was about to go (Luke 10:1). The seventy-two returned with joy, saying, "LORD (Yahweh), even the demons are subject to us in your name!" And he said to them, "I saw Satan fall like lightning from heaven. Behold, I have given you authority to tread on serpents and scorpions, and over all the power of the enemy, and nothing shall hurt you. Nevertheless, do not rejoice in this, that the spirits are subject to you, but rejoice that your names are written in heaven (Luke 10:17-20).*

I don't think we in the body of Christ know how many of us are hurting emotionally and are being tormented by demons. I do not think we really understand the influence the demons have on our minds and over us. Some people are into heavy sin and do not know they are in a battle for their very soul. Some are suffering and are afraid to tell someone of the battle they are going through. Because of lack of knowledge, we are often misdiagnosed with mental illness. In our natural world these phenomena need to be explained. We need to understand that the battle is in the mind.

Demons are real, and many people are suffering and in bondage because of them. However, I do not believe everything is a demon either. I remember when I first became a Christian some of the pastors were teaching on demons. It seemed that people took it to an extreme thinking everything that happened to them was demonic. My pastors at that time did not have all of the answers. Consequently, they stopped teaching on demons altogether.

When word got out that I was praying for people to be set free from the demonic, my phone started ringing off the hook. As I would answer, the person would say, "I have heard that you do deliverance and I really need help." It seemed it didn't matter how far they had to travel. In the early days of the ministry I was ministering in our home. As people would come into my living room and sit down I would ask a few questions about them and their history, so I could minister more effectively. After a short time, I would begin to pray for the individual. As I would start to pray, the demons in the person would start to manifest. I would start yelling, "the blood of Jesus." The more I yelled, "The blood," the more they manifested. I would become very frustrated, because the demons were not leaving.

While on the way to my home, the demons would begin to torment the person mentally. The demons did not want to be exposed. After I brought the person into my house, I would start praying for them, and the demons would manifest. The person would then begin to experience physical torment as well. It was very hard to watch these people suffer. These sessions would go on for two or three hours, sometimes longer. The person would make another appointment for the following week, and they would go through the manifestation all over again. Once the person would leave, my husband would say to me, "I thought you said you had authority, why won't the demons leave?" I would answer, "I don't know why. All I know is God said we were moving into deliverance and we did."

I began to fast and pray for days at a time. "Lord, You said I was going to move into deliverance and that I have authority over the demons. Why won't the demons leave? Lord, either deliver these people or take this ministry away from me." I couldn't bear to see the people in so much emotional and physical pain. It was truly heart breaking to see what these people would do to get free.

I called several of my Christian friends. I explained to them what the Lord told me about going into deliverance and how it started. However, I did not know what I was doing and I needed help. I then asked if they knew anyone that worked in deliverance. Most of them said, "No." However, one said, "Yes, there is a pastor that I know of in Ontario, California, that I heard does deliverance."

She gave me his information and I set up an appointment with him. I was so excited to meet him I could not wait. I knew he was going to have answers that I needed. I went to his church office and He said, "Oh, yes I used to do deliverance, but not anymore. My daughter is in the hospital very sick. She has been there for months. I believe it is because of the ministry of deliverance she is there. So I no longer do it. But there is a book you should read called, *This Presence Darkness*, by Frank Peretti. It will help you." I went right out and bought that book. I was very disappointed. Do not get me wrong. Frank Peretti did a great job of exposing how demons operate in the spiritual realm. However, it did not help me in my quest of casting demons out of people.

One day a man showed up at the church I was attending, and someone introduced him to me. Talking with him I found out he performed deliverances. Wow, that was awesome! He said he would mentor me. He did. We would set up an appointment with someone and the session would last all day, eight or nine hours. He mentored me for months. I took a lot of flack from other ministers at my church because some of the methods he was using did not seem to be very scriptural. One example he gave was angels dipping the demons in a Jacuzzi bath of blood until the demons did what the angels wanted. The people that spent hours in these sessions did not get much deliverance.

One morning in prayer, as I continued to seek answers, I asked the Lord to remove this call from my life. I did not feel like I could help these people. As soon as I asked for this to be removed from my life, the Lord brought to my remembrance a time when my youngest daughter Michelle had come into my bathroom. It was early morning, and I was getting ready for the day. I finished my shower and had blow-dried my hair. I was just starting to curl my hair with my curling iron, and set it down on the sink counter when my daughter Michelle reached up and grabbed it. Before I could reclaim it from her, she managed to get her little two-year-old fingers caught between the barrel and clamp. I couldn't get her fingers out of that curling iron fast enough. My heart was broken as tears ran down her cheeks and she screeched in pain.

41

I was holding her in my arms, crying out loud to God to stop the pain. We were very loud, between my cries and hers. I was surprised the neighbors did not call the police. Michelle must have cried for a half an hour. It is such a horrific emotion you feel when you see your child in so much pain and you cannot make it stop. The Lord spoke and said, "The emotions you felt for your child is how I feel when I see my children in pain." After he gave me this analogy, I was able to comprehend how He felt about the hurt and pain His children go through.

The Lord never intended for us to be so wounded. He has so much compassion for His children. He hears our cries and sees our tears. He told *Moses, And the Lord said: "I have surely seen the oppression of My people who are in Egypt, and have heard their cry because of their taskmasters, for I know their sorrows"* (Exodus 3:7). We also read, *Surely He has borne our grief and carried our sorrows; yet we esteemed Him stricken, smitten by God, and afflicted. But He was wounded for our transgressions, He was bruised for our iniquities; the chastisement for our peace was upon Him, and by His stripes we are healed. All we like sheep have gone astray; we have turned, every one, to his own way; and the Lord has laid on Him the iniquity of us all* (Isaiah 53:4-6).

My people are destroyed for lack of knowledge. Because you have rejected knowledge, I also will reject you from being priest for me; because you have forgotten the law of your God, I also will forget your children (Hosea 4:6). Many of us think we can live however we want, but we do not understand that we hurt ourselves and our children and future generations by not living God's way.

As I lay prostrated on the floor, in prayer before the Father, I repented of rejecting knowledge. I remembered that Paul said He prayed for the people he was writing to.

*That the God of Jesus the Father of glory, **may give to you the spirit of wisdom and revelation in the knowledge of Him, the eyes of your understanding being enlightened; that you may know what is the hope of His calling,** what are the riches of the glory of His inheritance in the saints, and what is the exceeding greatness of His power toward us who believe, according to the working of His mighty power which He worked in Christ when He raised Him from the dead and seated Him at His right hand in the heavenly places, far above all principality and power and might* *and dominion, and every name that is named, not only in this age but also in that which is to come. And He put all things under His feet, and gave Him to be head over all things to the church, which is His body, the fullness of Him who fills all in all* (Ephesians 1:17-23).

I started praying for the spirit of wisdom and revelation in the knowledge of Him—for His knowledge, wisdom, and understanding to set the captives free. I spent many hours on my face before the Lord, in prayer and fasting, seeking Him on behalf of the people.

Chapter 5

War in the Heavens

————❦❦❦————

*Y*ou may not realize it, but you are right in the middle of a great war. It's the war of the ages and the war, which has caused every other war in the history of humanity. It is the war between good and evil, between God and Satan, and you are right in the middle of it.

Ever since Satan fired the first shot against humanity in the Garden of Eden (Genesis 3), Adam and Eve and all their descendants have been held as prisoners of war in chains of slavery to sin, which keep us from our Heavenly Father. The chains of sin are a death sentence and cannot be broken by any human means.

There is, however, a way to be freed from the bonds of sin and join in the fight against evil: *Yeshua HaMoshiach* (the Messiah). Only *Yeshua* can free us from our captivity to sin. Under His command, we can become active soldiers for His Kingdom, working to free countless of other POWs. Make no mistake: You ARE part of this war.

There are two spiritual kingdoms: a heavenly kingdom under God's rule and an earthly (worldly) kingdom under Satan's rule. Satan rebelled against God and he was kicked out of heaven: *How art thou fallen from heaven, O Lucifer, son of the morning! How art thou cut down to the ground, which didst weaken the nations! For thou hast said in thine heart, I will ascend into heaven, I will exalt my throne above the stars of God: I will sit also upon the mount of the congregation, in the sides of the north: I will ascend above the heights of the clouds; I will be like the Most High. Yet thou shalt be brought down to hell, to the sides of the pit* (Isaiah 14:12-15).

These two kingdoms are at war. We read, *... we do not wrestle against flesh and blood, but against principalities, against powers, against the rulers of the darkness of this age, against spiritual hosts of wickedness in the heavenly places* (Ephesians 6:12). We also read, *And the dragon was enraged with the woman, and he went to make war with the rest of her offspring, who keep the commandments of God and have the testimony of Jesus* (Revelation 12:17). This refers to Israel and to followers of *Yeshua* who are grafted into Israel. Satan hates us because of *Yeshua* and he knows his time is short.

When a person chooses to become a believer in *Yeshua* and accepts Him as Lord, it means stepping out of Satan's spiritual kingdom of darkness and the bondage of sin that is within that kingdom, and stepping into God's kingdom of light and separation from sin. It means stepping away from an evil spiritual world that is in general rebellion against God and living in God's spiritual realm where we are obedient to Him.

In his letter to the church at Colosse, Paul states that *Yeshua* delivered us out of Satan's spiritual power and enabled us to step into His spiritual kingdom. *He has rescued us from the domain of darkness and transferred us into the Kingdom of his dear Son. It is through his Son that we have redemption — that is, our sins have been forgive*(Colossians 1:13-15).

Paul again states this in his letter to the church at Galatia when he said that we are able to leave our evil world through the death of *Yeshua*. *Grace to you and peace from God the Father and our Lord Jesus Christ, who gave Himself for our sins, that He might deliver us from this present evil age, according to the will of our God and Father* (Galatians 1:3-4).

Even though Yeshua lived in the world, He demonstrated His spiritual dominion over it and His ability to influence it and change it. He demonstrated through word and action to people around Him, while living in a physical body, what it was like to live in God's spiritual kingdom. When *Yeshua*, during His life on earth, preached the good news about God's spiritual kingdom, the miracles, deliverance and changed lives, were evidence of God's kingdom touching this earth through His life. *Jesus answered and said to him, "Most assuredly, I say to you, unless one is born again, he cannot see the kingdom of God* (John 3:3).

When we receive *Yeshua* as our Lord and Savior, we repent of our sins and ask Him to come into our heart. When this happens, the Holy Spirit becomes alive in us and our spirit becomes alive toward God. This is what we call salvation, and being born again. The Hebrew word for "to save" is *Yasha*`, to save, be saved, be delivered, to give victory to.

Through *Yeshua's* life, death, and resurrection, God provided a means for ordinary people to enter into a spiritual life where the kingdom of God could be established spiritually within us.

Living in God's spiritual kingdom means that we must accept Him as Supreme Ruler. We must obey His commands in the same way we would if we lived in a kingdom on earth and had to choose to obey the earthly king or queen's commands or suffer the consequences.

The kingdom comes upon us through the restoration of relationship with God and the presence of the Holy Spirit in our lives. The power of the kingdom is demonstrated in lives that are transformed and in souls that are restored to what God had initially intended them to be.

Believers continue to live in the world, which is separated from God, under the spiritual rule of Satan and under the physical dominion of people who are generally separated from God. But, believers no longer want to be controlled by the world's influences.

Of course, this does not mean that we can no longer live in the world. That is clearly impossible. It does mean that we are meant to be very different in our thinking, emotions, words and actions from all other people who are not believers. In this way, believers are in the world but not of it. We see in the book of John, *Yeshua* prayed for believers:

I have given them Your word; and the world has hated them because they are not of the world, just as I am not of the world. I do not pray that You should take them out of the world, but that You should keep them from the evil one. They are not of the world, just as I am not of the world. Sanctify them by Your truth. Your word is truth. As You sent Me into the world, I also have sent them into the world (John 17:14-18).

One day I had a vision while in prayer with the Lord. The setting was around the 1800s. I saw a beautiful horse drawn buggy. In the buggy I saw a wealthy man. The buggy was clopping down a cobblestone street. He happened to come upon a group of slaves on the right hand side of the street. They were chained to a metal stake in the ground. The chains were so short, the slaves could not stand up. They had to stoop down or sit on the ground. As this wealthy man approached them, he noticed they had been badly beaten. They had bruises and scars all over their bodies. Some had been branded. They had also been starved; their ribs and bones could be seen. They looked like walking skeletons. Their clothing was a shred of fabric, barely covering their bony bodies. The wealthy man's heart was broken and filled with compassion seeing such human suffering.

How could anyone treat people like this? He went to the slave owner and asked, "How much do you want for all of your slaves?" The wicked slave master laughed a hideous laugh. He knew he had so abused these slaves physically, emotionally, and sexually, that they had become worthless. He sneered out an outrageous price. The price he gave was hundreds more than what any slave was worth. The compassion that the wealthy man felt for those slaves was so overwhelming that he paid the price to set the slaves free.

Each deal had to be closed legally. When a slave was set free, legal documents called manumission papers were necessary. The rich man paid the purchase price and signed the necessary documents. When the transaction was complete, he went to the slaves and presented the documents to them. He told them they were free. No man could ever own them again.

The slaves could not believe what just happened. For years they dreamt of freedom. Some even tried to escape, but they were caught, beaten and locked up. They were so excited that they congregated onto the street. They had great joy. They danced, sang, and laughed. It felt so good to stand up straight. They talked for several hours about how this man just came by and paid the price for their freedom. They were overwhelmed with great joy. However, as night started to fall, they did not know what to do. They had never been free before. Even though they had always wanted freedom and they dreamt of it, they didn't know what to do with their newfound freedom. As the darkness rolled in, one by one, each slave went back to the place they had been chained and put themselves back in the chains that had bound them.

The Lord told me this is what we do as believers. The wealthy man represents *Yeshua*. He has such compassion on us. He sees our slave owner Satan has beaten us down. *Yeshua* has paid the price to buy us. He paid with His own blood. However, some do not know what to do with this newfound freedom. Oh yes, we all get excited when we first receive Christ as our Lord and savior. But, as spiritual darkness falls, some don't know how to walk in this freedom. Because of lack of knowledge, we can put ourselves back into bondage.

How do we walk in the kingdom of God? How do we walk in this freedom when we have never walked this way before?

We are a soul and spirit housed in a body

When God created us in His image He created us as a soul and spirit in a body. We are created in the image of God. *Then God said, "Let Us make man in Our image, according to Our likeness"* (Genesis 1:26). Satan hates God. In this war, Satan hates and wants to distort the image of God in us. He does this by battering and bruising our soul realm.

When we accept *Yeshua* as Lord, our spirits become born again. Nevertheless, our soul needs to be restored, and our flesh needs to be crucified. *For the word of God is living and powerful, and sharper than any two-edged sword, piercing even to the division of soul and spirit, and of joints and marrow, and is a discerner of the thoughts and intents of the heart* (Hebrews 4:12).

The Greek word used for soul is *psyche*. The soul is the "psychological" nature of man, including our **mind**, **emotions** and **will**. God wants to heal and restore our souls, as He did with David's, for His namesake and glory. *He restores my soul; He leads me in the paths of righteousness for His name's sake* (Psalm 23:3).

*Now may the God of peace Himself **sanctify** you completely; and may your whole **spirit, soul, and body** be preserved blameless at the coming of our Lord Jesus Christ* (I Thessalonians 5:23).

The Hebrew word for sanctification is *Qadash*. It means to consecrate, sanctify, prepare, dedicate, be hallowed, be holy, be sanctified, and be separate. To sanctify is literally "to set apart for special use or purpose," figuratively "to make holy or sacred," act of making holy, consecration; process of becoming holy; purification, act of making free from sin. He is sanctifying us to set us apart for His kingdom. In the kingdom of God there is also restoration; *And that He may send Jesus Christ, who was preached to you before, whom heaven must receive until the times of restoration of all things, which God has spoken by the mouth of all His holy prophets since the world began* (Acts 3: 20,21). Part of the restoration process is restoring our battered soul (mind, emotion and will).

After we accept *Yeshua* as Lord, we cannot be possessed, because we are blood bought and paid for in full by *Yeshua's* atoning work at Calvary.

God explained it to me like this: A homeowner owns the deed to their house. If that house gets termites, it doesn't mean the termites own the house. However, they can destroy the foundation of that house. It is the same with demons. They cannot possess the believer but they can infest the soul realm and destroy the foundation.

Part of the sanctification and restoration process of our soul is renewing our mind. Our mind is the battlefield where the battle with Satan and demons take place. Satan uses our mind by putting thoughts in it.

We read, *And do not be conformed to this world, but be **transformed** by the renewing of your mind that you may prove what is that good and acceptable and perfect will of God* (Romans 12:2).

The word *transformation* in Webster's dictionary means: *To change the form or appearance of, to change the condition, character, or function of.*

Then we read, *For though we walk in the flesh, we do not war according to the flesh. For the weapons of our warfare are not carnal but mighty in God for pulling down strongholds, casting down arguments and every high thing that exalts itself against the knowledge of God, bringing **every thought** into captivity to the obedience of Christ* (II Corinthians 10:3-5).

Our thoughts are crucial, because they are the first to be triggered in the chain reaction of our souls. Our thoughts stir up our emotions; our emotions then influence our desires; and our desires are what produce our actions. This is why it's so very important to take every thought captive. If we do this, then we will be able to prevent that chain reaction before it even begins.

*This I say, therefore, and testify in the LORD (Yahweh), that you should no longer walk as the rest of the Gentiles walk, **in the futility of their mind, having their understanding darkened,** being alienated from the life of God (Elohim), because of the igno-rance that is in them, because of the blindness of their heart; who, being past feeling, have given themselves over to lewdness, to work all uncleanness with greediness. But you have not so learned Christ, if indeed you have heard Him and have been taught by Him, as the truth is in Yeshua: that you put off, concerning your former conduct, the old man which grows corrupt according to the deceitful lusts, and be **renewed in the spirit of your mind**, and **that you put on***

the new man which was created according to God (Elohim), in true righteousness and holiness (Ephesians 4: 17- 24).

Paul uses a very descriptive word picture of this change. First, we should not allow ourselves to be poured into the world's mold. This will only cause us to look like the world, to act like the world and to talk like the world. Instead we should be transformed by renewing our minds with what God has said. Imagine a caterpillar as he turns into a butterfly. This transformation is what Paul is talking about.

Yeshua said in John, *You will know the truth, and the truth will set you free (John 8:32)*. Being free is not automatic. First you must understand that the truth is what makes you free and to be free you have to know what the truth is Later in John, *Yeshua* was praying for his disciples, he said, *"Sanctify them by the truth; your word is truth."* (John 17:17). *Yeshua* said *your word is truth,* so knowing and understanding God's word is what brings about our sanctification and knowing this truth will set you free.

How do we renew our mind? We need to read the Bible. The Bible tells us do not be just a hearer of the word, but a doer of the word.

But be doers of the word, and not hearers only, deceiving yourselves. For if anyone is a hearer of the word and not a doer, he is like a man observing his natural face in a mirror; for he observes himself, goes away, and immediately forgets what kind of man he was. But he who looks into the perfect law of liberty and continues in it, and is not a forgetful hearer but a doer of the work, this one will be blessed in what he does (James 1:22-25).

In this process our emotions need to be healed.

Chapter 6

What is Inner Healing?

---

he term "inner healing" is a modern phrase that describes what the Holy Spirit is doing in these last days. It is emotional healing. Inner healing does not erase a memory or change our personal history. It brings comfort from the Holy Spirit in the area of emotional pain. It enables us to have compassion and prepares us to minister to all who have suffered in the same way, just as Christ suffered for us at Calvary. We read *Blessed be the God and Father of our Lord Jesus Christ, the Father of mercies and God of all comfort, who comforts us in all our tribulation, that we may be able to comfort those who are in any trouble, with the comfort with which we ourselves are comforted by God. For as the sufferings of Christ abound in us, so our consolation also abounds through Christ* (II Corinthians 1:3-5). God's word will never change. *Jesus Christ is the same yesterday, today, and forever* (Hebrews 13:8).

Yeshua proclaims liberty to those who are bound and the opening of the prison doors to those who are captive. It is the Father's will that you be healed emotionally, that you be delivered, and that your soul be restored. *...He has sent Me to heal the brokenhearted, to proclaim liberty to the captives, and the opening of the prison to those who are bound* (Isaiah 61:1).

Then Yeshua returned in the power of the Spirit to Galilee, and news of Him went out through all the surrounding region. And He taught in their synagogues, being glorified by all. So He came to Nazareth, where He had been brought up. And as His custom was, He went into the synagogue on the Sabbath day, and stood up to read. And He was handed the book of the prophet Isaiah. And when He had opened the book, He found the place where it was written: 'The Spirit of the LORD (Yahweh) is upon Me, because He has anointed Me to preach the gospel to the poor; He has sent Me to heal the brokenhearted, to proclaim liberty to the captives and recovery of sight to the blind, to set at liberty those who are oppressed; to proclaim the acceptable year of the Lord (Luke 4:14-19).

And He began to say to them, "Today this Scripture is fulfilled in your hearing" (Luke 4:21)

Luke 4 is the fulfillment of Isaiah 61. Isaiah 61 was written to Israel after the children of Israel had gone through so much pain and suffering. It was their disobedience that caused their enemy to be able to overtake them. They went after other gods to serve them and the word says they committed spiritual adultery. When we read the Bible, we can see how much God loves Israel, even after all of their sin. Their sin is what caused the pain. I can see that the disobedience to God's word (His loving instructions), knowing or unknowing, in my ancestors, parents and my own life, is what caused all of my emotional pain.

Then He said to them, "These are the words which I spoke to you while I was still with you, that all things must be fulfilled which were written in the Law of Moses, the Prophets, and the Psalms (Luke 24:44). *Yeshua* was referring to the Old Testament prophecy concerning Him.

We also read in Isaiah, *Instead of your shame you shall have double honor, and instead of confusion they shall rejoice in their portion. Therefore in their land they shall possess double; everlasting joy shall be theirs* (Isaiah 61:7). A lot of us grow up with shame because of how we were raised and the things we have done. I know I had a lot of shame. When the Lord was healing me He took that shame and He has given me double honor and joy.

We are in a spiritual war that started in the Garden of Eden. Satan deliberately wounds our hearts and causes us to become prisoners of war. He puts us into an emotional prison house, so we will not be effective for the Kingdom of God.

Some of the bars that hold us in this prison are: hurt, rejection, abandonment, unforgiveness, anger, rage, hatred, resentment, fear, doubt, unworthiness, guilt, sadness, victimization, loneliness, despair, discouragement, self-pity, depression, isolation, loss, inadequacy, shame, guilt, hopelessness, offense, exhaustion, death, murder, suicidal thoughts, and nothingness.

One day, when I was still ministering out of my home and the Lord was teaching me about deliverance, a woman called me from Santa Barbara, California. She had heard about the ministry from a family member and knew she needed deliverance. She had been going into trancelike states and attacking her 6"4' live-in boyfriend of many years. In this trancelike state, she would try to kill him. He told me she would attack and start choking him. At other times she would come at him with a knife. She weighed only ninety-five pounds. When in a trance state, she would become strong. He would have to fight for his life. Many times the police were called. He would go to jail, because they would not believe she attacked him first.

When I started praying for her, we could feel the presence of the Holy Spirit. As the Holy Spirit became stronger, she fell to the ground under the power of God. As I continued praying for her, a demon manifested. Her body and face were contorting, as she writhed in agonizing pain on my living room floor. My heart swelled with compassion for her. I was screaming at the demon, "In the name of Jesus you have to leave." The demon started yelling back, "No." This continued for several hours. I was exhausted. Every muscle in my body was tense and hurting. I was getting nowhere.

The louder my voice got the louder the demon got. Nothing that I said to the demon made a difference. Out of sheer exhaustion, I stopped yelling at the demon and started praying, more like pleading for an answer, and asking God "What do you want me to do?" The Lord told me, "Read Isaiah 61."

I responded, "I already read that... What else do you want me to do?"

Again He told me, "Read Isaiah 61." I kept insisting I had already read it!

This went on for a few minutes, until I read it again, "The Spirit of the Lord God *is* upon Me, because the Lord has anointed Me to preach good tidings to the poor; He has sent Me to heal the brokenhearted, to proclaim liberty to the captives, and the opening of the prison to *those who are* bound." The Lord said, "I wrote it that way. It says to heal her broken heart (first) to set her free." As I received this understanding of His word I began to pray that her heart would be healed. She started crying very hard. The Lord was healing her. The demon lost its power and the battle was won. I found out later that her father abused her horribly: verbally, physically and sexually.

Our Father is very gracious. When He starts healing us, He takes a layer at a time. Some of us have had so much hurt that we could not bear all of it coming up at one time. For some of us, that can take some time. For me it was several years.

When He is healing us, I believe he allows circumstances to be in our lives that press into those areas of pain. Many times we react with great anger not knowing why. The last thing I was healed of had to do with food. Due to my parents' alcoholism there was little money for our basic needs. However, I did not know I needed more healing. I thought the LORD (*Yahweh*) had healed me completely.

When I was pregnant with our daughter Michelle, I gained a lot of weight. This was a result of bed rest due to a high-risk pregnancy. I was trying to watch what I ate. One night, I wanted something sweet. Instead of getting something that was bad for me, I decided to eat fruit. I went to the refrigerator for some grapes.

Benjamin came in and asked, "What are you eating?"

I answered, "Grapes, would you like some?"

He said, in a very sarcastic way, "No, not now...You and the kids eat everything good in the house and I don't get anything... How long have we had grapes?" He was very irate.

I said, "Since I went shopping last."

He asked, "Why didn't you tell me we had grapes?" I was confused. I did not know how to answer him. I was thinking, "What did he want a grocery list on the refrigerator door of everything I buy at the store? Why hadn't he looked to see what we had?" I started feeling myself getting upset and very angry.

When I would get hurt emotionally or angry, I would not be able to talk. Growing up, I had no "voice." It would feel like I had the wind knocked out of me. At this point in our marriage, I was learning how to communicate. Benjamin is a great communicator. He had helped me open up. He would encourage me to talk to him and let him know how I felt. So, I went over to the couch where he was sitting and I sat down on the other end facing him. I thought to myself, "This is great." I started telling him how I felt. I said, "I didn't like the way you talked to me, it was very hurtful."

I was so happy I was able to tell him how I felt. But it did not go the way I thought it should. He again, in a very angry sarcastic voice, said to me, "How do you think I feel? I give you money for food and I don't get anything. You don't think about me." That was it! What he said was not true. I became very angry. I was spitting fire. I waddled my pregnant body upstairs thinking, "That's it, tomorrow I am moving out and getting a job. I will never take any of his money again." It didn't matter that I was seven and half months pregnant, it was a high risk pregnancy and I had to stay off of my feet.

In my past I would run away from situations instead of dealing with them. The only problem was, they would come with me.

As the anger raged inside of me I asked the Lord where this anger was coming from. In an instance the Lord showed me a situation that happened when I was a little girl of maybe three or four at the oldest. One day, three of my siblings and I were sitting on the floor eating a bag of potato chips. This was a rare

Physically running away is a commonly used option for people that have emotional wounds. Some people will move to another location thinking their problems will be left behind. Others will jump from job to job in an attempt to find a company that isn't filled with people they don't like. A third approach is frequently changing relationships in search of a situation that doesn't have any problems. Problems are often caused, or occurred by, how you act and who you are. Therefore, they will follow you wherever you go. There are some problems that may be solved by changing your location. However, if you find that you encounter similar problems wherever you go, running is obviously not the answer.

treat for us. My mother was standing over us yelling, "You little pigs! You eat everything in this house."

When the Lord brought this to my remembrance, I started crying. There was so much emotional pain attached to that memory. I did not have a memory of this until that night. All through my life, in situations where someone would make a rude remark about someone eating, it would upset me. If anyone called someone a pig for eating something, I would want to come out of my skin. I never thought about these responses. They were normal to me. I had not put the two together until that night. I cried for forty-five minutes as the memory surfaced. I could not believe there was more to be healed.

After the Lord healed this area, all the anger I had towards Benjamin was gone. I had such sweet peace. I asked the Lord why He had not healed me all at once. He said, "You could not have taken all of the pain surfacing all at one time. You just cried for forty-five minutes from one memory. Your heart would not be able to handle all the hurt at one time." *He who has begun a good work in you will complete it until the day of Jesus Christ"*(Philippians 1:6). Instead of going downstairs and talking to Benjamin, I fell into a deep sleep.

The next morning, when I awoke, Benjamin was already awake and downstairs. I went downstairs where he was sitting at the kitchen table. I shared with him what the Lord had revealed to me and how He healed me. He took me in his arms, held me close, and said, "I am so sorry, sweetheart. I knew you had it bad growing up, but I didn't know how bad it really was."

I told him, "I know now why so many people get divorced. They have hurts and pains which aren't healed." I call these areas puss pockets. Many times couples are not dealing with the situation that is in front of them, but something that is buried from their past, that they might not even be aware of. When one of these puss pockets gets touched it brings anger or other emotions. For me, when one of my puss pockets would get touched, the anger was over the top. It would feel like a volcano would erupt inside of my heart. Then my mind would start thinking all kinds of crazy thoughts. My mind would vacillate: anger, hatred, hopelessness, discouragement, rejection, self-rejection, beating myself up verbally, wanting to run, wanting to die, etc.

From Benjamin's perspective, on the night of the grapes issue, he felt that I didn't care for him. Since that night we have learned there are five love languages. Benjamin's love language is acts of service. Since I did not offer him grapes he thought I had not thought of him. He felt rejected and unloved by me. Consequently, he was hurt and angry.

Just as the grape issue came up for me, you might find areas of your life where something happens and all of a sudden your emotions feel like a volcano going off inside of you. There is overreaction to a situation, even if you do not know you are overreacting. You might feel like running from the situation. You might feel really angry. Maybe the thoughts start going through your mind as they did mine. You might become hypervigilant, your adrenalin might kick in, you cannot sleep, etc.

What does a person do when this happens?

Get away with the Lord. Go somewhere you can be alone and quiet. Ask the Father where this is coming from. Be still and let him show you if this has a root somewhere in your past, or if this is a puss pocket. If He brings up a memory from your past, as He did in me, invite Him in to heal it. You may feel like crying. Do not stop the tears. Let them come as the emotion is surfacing. Sometimes writing about your childhood or past is a way to let the memories, pain, and emotions come up to the surface, so they can be healed. I believe that God gave us the ability to bury the pain until we bring that pain to the cross and let Him heal it. If we try to deal with the hurt without the cross and the work of *Yeshua*, all we have is the memory and the pain of that memory. As believers, we can allow our Father access to our puss pockets. He then takes the pain and heals us.

Prayer:

Father, show me if there are any hurts and pain in my life that I have buried that need to be healed. Are there any puss pockets in me? (If He shows you any areas. Take it to Him) Father, show me where you were when I was going through this. Please heal this area of my life. I give it to you and I apply the blood of the lamb to the pain. In Yeshua's name, Amen!

In the process of God healing our soul, not only does our mind need to be renewed by His word, and our emotions healed, but also our will needs to line up to the Father's will.

Not everyone who says to Me, 'Lord, Lord' shall enter the kingdom of heaven, but he who does the will of My Father in heaven (Matthew 7:21).

Chapter 7

The Father's Will

—⚜—

For many years I never thought about what God wanted. I wanted my will to be done and not God's. When God first started teaching me about "Thy will be done," he did it in a great way. When I felt Benjamin was going to ask me to marry him I started looking for wedding rings. I had already been married twice, and I could not find any rings that I liked. I was looking at rings in the two hundred dollar range. I gave up and told the Lord He was going to have to pick them out. I could not find anything I liked. I prayed, "Lord you know the rings you want me to have, let them be your will." At the time I prayed this, I was really not thinking about God's perfect will for my wedding rings.

Soon after this prayer, Benjamin invited me to go on a skiing trip for the Police Winter Olympics that he was participating in. It was held in February at Lake Tahoe, California. The last day we were there we went up to a little restaurant overlooking Heavenly Lake. As we were sitting there enjoying cheesecake and a cup of coffee, he brought out a card and in the card he asked if I would marry him. Of course I said, "Yes." He reached into his pocket and pulled out my rings. They were the most beautiful rings I had ever seen. The cost was in the thousands not hundreds. The center diamond in the ring is a marquise, my favorite cut.

The Lord started showing me, just as I was looking for two hundred dollar rings, that some of us have a poverty mentality. Many times he has so much more for us than what we could ever think or ask.

After we got married, we lived in the home that Benjamin had purchased before I met him. It was a three-bedroom, two-bath house. I was so thankful to have a home. However, when he bought it, he bought it for an investment. Because it was an investment property, it was in great need of some TLC. I had my heart set on a new home. We started looking. At the time, houses were increasing in value. It was one of the times real estate bubbled in Southern California.

Benjamin was good to me. He wanted to give me my heart's desire. As we were looking for a new home, I found a new housing community I thought we could afford. However, this community would have added an hour to Benjamin's already hour and a half commute (on a good day in Los Angeles traffic) to work. I tried to convince Benjamin that it would be a great investment. In my heart I just wanted a new house. I did not think about anything else. I convinced Benjamin to put a deposit down on a new house. He did not feel that it was a wise choice, since there would be an extra hour added to his commute. I remember praying and claiming that house.

Benjamin had talked about changing positions within the Sheriff's Department. This would change the location he was working and possibly bring him closer to the area we wanted to live, I was thinking God could move his job closer. I did not realize it was not that simple. I had been under the teaching that you lay hands on something and claim it. I had also been taught that wherever your foot treads is yours. Therefore, as a good faithful Christian, I believed that house was mine in *Yeshua's* name.

As time went on, it became clear that my husband did not want to have a three to four hour commute. He asked me to pray about it again. After he left for work, I got down on my knees before God and started praying about the house. Again, I was claiming it and thanking God wherever my foot treads is mine. The Lord started speaking to me. He said, "Stop it! This is not faith, it is manipulation. You have been trying to manipulate your husband and Me. This house is not for you and I want you to stop this right now." I was shocked. I could strongly feel the presence of His Holy Spirit on me. The Spirit brought correction and a spirit of repentance. I was overwhelmed with regret as the Lord showed me that what I was doing was not of faith. I had to call my husband. When I called him the Spirit of repentance was strong on me. I was crying and telling my husband I was very sorry and the house was not for us, and that God had spoken to me and told me to stop it. I had asked for his forgiveness. My husband was shocked. Up to that point I would say God told me this, or God told me that and he would say, "Quit telling people God speaks to you, they are going to think you're crazy. No one hears from God." After this he believed I heard from God.

I gave up the thought of a new house. I started thanking the Lord for the one I had. Two years later, I was in prayer about the repairs the house needed. The Lord told me to pray for a new home. I argued I did not need one and anyway they were too expensive. Again, He said, "Pray for a new house." So I did. After prayer I opened up the newspaper and the prices of houses had dropped.

The Lord opened the door for us to get into a beautiful home, which was much more beautiful than the house I wanted in the first place.

When we moved into the new house we found that the owners had bought it two years earlier and put $100,000 of upgrades in the house. During this time there had been a crash in the U.S. economy because gas prices were going up. The people that we bought the house from owned a trucking company, and the owners were selling their house in fear of rising gas prices. We were able to buy the house at an incredibly low price.

The Lord started making it very clear to me that He has plans to bless us. Many times we want our will to be done and not His will to be done.

I started praying, "Lord, let my will lineup with your will and only your will." As I did this, He started showing me other things where my will had not lined up with His will.

It is bigger than material things. It is very important in these last days that our will line up with His will. Christ is the head of the body. The body needs to follow the will of the head. We need to be guided by His eye not a bit in our mouth.

I will instruct you and teach you in the way you should go; I will guide you with My eye. Do not be like the horse or like the mule, which have no understanding, which must be harnessed with bit and bridle, else they will not come near you. Many sorrows shall be to the wicked; but he who trusts in the LORD (Yahweh), mercy shall surround him (Psalm 32:8-10).

Prayer:

Father, Line my will up to your will, I want to be guided by your eye and not by a bit in my mouth, in Yeshua's name, Amen.

Chapter 8

Our Flesh needs to be Crucified

―――᪥――

long with our will becoming the Father's will, our flesh needs to be crucified. The flesh is the part of us that resists our transformation into the new person in Christ. Furthermore, since this is the case, the devil wants to use the pleasures of our flesh to keep us enslaved to our old habits and sinful attitudes.

We have daily choices to live according to God's righteous desires, and deny sin. When we use our power to choose God's way instead of sin's way, we crucify our flesh.

I say then: Walk in the Spirit, and you shall not fulfill the lust of the flesh. For the flesh lusts against the Spirit, and the Spirit against the flesh; and these are contrary to one another, so that you do not do the things that you wish. But if you are led by the Spirit, you are not under the law. Now the works of the flesh are evident, which are: adultery, fornication, uncleanness, lewdness, idolatry, sorcery, hatred, contentions, jealousies, outbursts of wrath, selfish ambitions, dissensions, heresies, envy, murders, drunkenness, revelries, and the like; of which I tell you beforehand, just as I also told you in time past, that those who practice such things will not inherit the kingdom of God (Elohim). But the fruit of the Spirit is love, joy, peace, long-suffering, kindness, goodness, faithfulness, gentleness, and self-control. Against such there is no law. And those who are Christ's have crucified the flesh with its passions and desires. If we live in the Spirit, let us also walk in the Spirit. Let us not become conceited, provoking one another, envying one another (Galatians 5:16-26).

*Forasmuch then as Christ hath suffered for us in the flesh, arm yourselves likewise with the same mind: for he that hath suffered in the flesh hath ceased from sin; that he **no longer should live the rest of his time in the flesh to the lusts of men, but to the will of God*** (I Peter 4:1-2). (emphasis added)

When a man is crucified, he dies. When he dies, he is dead. Therefore those of us who belong to *Yeshua* need to crucify the flesh so that we become dead to the flesh, dead to our passions, and dead to our desires. *And those who are Christ's have crucified the flesh with its passions and desires* (Galatians 5: 24). *I have been crucified with Christ and I no longer live, but Christ lives in me. The life I live in the body, I live by faith in the Son of God (Elohim), who loved me and gave himself for me* (Galatians 2:20)

We need to commit to responding to the flesh differently than we used to, by choosing to be a Living sacrifice to God and by being obedient to him.

But put on the Lord Jesus Christ, and make not provision for the flesh, to fulfill the lusts thereof (Romans 13:14).

When a situation came up and I knew I had to crucify my flesh, in my mind's eye I could see a fork in the road. I had a choice to go in one of two paths. The path of my flesh or the path that God wanted for me. Normally, I would flippantly make decisions based on my feelings. I would come to this fork in the road and my flesh would want to take the path of sin. This time, I would stop and ask the Lord what He wanted me to do. He would show me He wanted me to take the path of righteousness. I would feel this fight inside of me. It was such a tug of war.

My old nature of sin did not want to die. The Lord then gave me understanding. He showed me when I was on the path I put myself on, following my sinful flesh and the temptation of Satan, there were time bomb curses that would go off. On this path, everything would seem to fall apart or my decisions would make my life miserable. At the end of sin there is always a price to pay. Sin is not for our pleasure, but for our destruction. However, when I chose His paths, He said there were time bomb blessings.

These blessing would come upon me and overtake me. They would chase me down. I could not get away from them.

Satan lied to me by communicating that I would not have any more fun if I surrendered all of me to my Heavenly Father. Then the Lord showed me that, through my sin, I was coming out from underneath God's protection. I was in Satan's territory. It was as though Satan was taking a baseball bat, hitting me in the head with it, telling me how much fun the sin was, and how much I enjoyed it. The truth was, sin caused a great deal of suffering to myself and those around me.

Crucifying your flesh does not mean that your life will lack pleasure. God is the author of true pleasure that is not tainted with sin in any way. In fact, God provides perfect pleasures that bring lasting satisfaction and joy, unlike the temporary pleasures that selfish sin offers.

The Lord has shown me that we need to repent of the sins we have committed in the flesh in order to be forgiven.

Come now, and let us reason together, says the Lord, "Though your sins are like scarlet, they shall be as white as snow; though they are red like crimson, they shall be as wool" (Isaiah 1:18).

Prayer of Repentance

Father, I humble myself before You today. I repent today of all my sins. Cause me to hate sin the way You hate sin. Let me see sin the way You see it. I ask that the Holy Spirit would convict me of my sin and show me the areas of my life that are unpleasing to You. I want to have a change of heart and a change of mind. I want Your heart and Your mind to be in me. I want to serve You, Father. I ask that You would wash me with the blood of *Yeshua* and cleanse me so that I would be a holy vessel, pleasing unto You, in *Yeshua*'s name, Amen.

Chapter 9

Moving beyond Rejection and Abandonment into Forgiveness

―――✦―――

Two of the strategies that Satan uses to wound our hearts are rejection and abandonment. Rejection and abandonment keep love away from us. When we feel rejected, we put walls up around our heart so we won't get hurt. This is to keep love from coming in and love from going out. We might say things like, "No one wants me...I will never love again... No one will ever get my heart again... They will never hurt me again..." We behave in ways that cause people to reject us. Or, because we feel rejected by others, we reject others first and sometimes we even reject ourselves.

Rejection is one of Satan's best forms of oppression. Rejection may keep people from coming to God for salvation or keep them from reaching their full potential with God. It distorts our image of God as a loving heavenly Father who is a lover of our soul.

It also undermines, breaks, or prevents normal and harmonious relations between family members, spouses, fellow believers, co-workers and friends.

I told you earlier about the woman at a women's retreat who had built walls up around her heart because of the pain of rejection and abandonment as a child.

Symptoms of rejection and abandonment are: feeling unloved, unable to accept love, unable to give love, self–rejection, feel abandoned, starvation for love, can't love spouse/children, self-hate, feel worthless, fear of rejection, believe yourself to be a failure, agony within, feel inferior, low self-image, feel insecure, withdrawn personality, self condemning, tries to please others, seek approval, internal hurt/pain, depression, and doing things that cause others to reject them.

Rejection, whether active or passive, real or imaginary, robs *Yeshua* of His rightful position as Lord in our lives. Rejection keeps believers from experiencing the vitality and quality of life He alone gives. Satan knows the more love we have the more faith we have.

When God started to heal me of all the rejection in my life, He showed me this scripture: *Blessed be the God and Father of our Lord Jesus Christ, who has blessed us with every spiritual blessing in the heavenly places in Christ. Just as he chose us in him before the foundation of the world, that we should be holy and without blame before him in love: having predestined us to adoption as sons by Jesus Christ to himself, according to the good pleasure of his will, to the praise of the glory of his grace by which He made us accepted in the Beloved,* (Ephesians 1:3-6).

I must have read it a hundred times. I was not rejected. I was accepted and adopted by my Heavenly Father. (*Merriam-Webster*, **adopt:** to take by choice into a relationship; *especially*: to take voluntarily (a child of other parents) as one's own child.)

The word that's translated here "has made us accepted" is the verb that's derived from the Greek noun for grace, which is *charis*. And the same word is used when the angel Gabriel saluted Mary and said, "Hail thou that art highly favored." It's a very strong word. We need to understand that God does not simply tolerate us; His favor is upon us. He is passionately committed to us.

If you have lived your life feeling rejected and/or abandoned, would you pray this prayer right now?

Father, thank you I am not rejected or abandoned. I am accepted in the Beloved and you have never forsaken me. You have adopted me through the blood of your son. You are my Father. You truly love me and I am your child. I belong to the best family in the world. I am a child of the King of kings, in the name of *Yeshua* of Nazareth, Amen.

Unforgiveness

Forgiveness of others is a gift we give ourselves. Someone once said, "Unforgiveness is like drinking poison and hoping the other person dies."

Forgiveness is often an important part of deliverance. Every demon within a person has a legal right before God to be there. Satan is a legalist and knows "his rights" before God to send demons into a person. Satan works like a lawyer, demanding his rights before God. *Yeshua* is our advocate, who also defends our rights before God. We need to take away the demons' legal rights, so we can cast them out.

We need to forgive those who treat us badly. *But I tell you: Love your enemies and pray for those who persecute you that you may be sons of your Father in heaven* (Matthew 5:44-45a). Sometimes we are afraid to forgive, because we think we have to tolerate abuse. Forgiveness is not letting the offense recur again and again. We don't have to tolerate, nor should we keep ourselves open to, any form of abuse. While God commands us to forgive others, He never told us to trust those who violated our trust or that we have to have them in our lifes.

It is difficult to forgive in our own strength. It seems a difficult concept to understand. We want, instead, to see justice done for the harm done to us. Forgiveness is surrenduring to God, the right to take care of justice. By refusing to transfer the right of exact punishment or revenge to God we are telling Him we don't trust Him to take care of matters.

When the Lord started healing me, one of the things I had to do was forgive. I had to forgive my parents for not keeping me safe. I had to let go of my bitterness towards them. Then I had to forgive my brother-in-law for molesting me and robbing me of my innocence.

When I was around forty-five years old and married to Benjamin, I received a phone call from my ex-brother-in-law. When I heard his voice on the other end of the receiver, my heart started beating very fast, and my thoughts started racing. I wondered how he had gotten my number and why was he calling me. He said he had become a Christian. He was calling to ask my forgiveness for the harm he had done to me. He had stolen my innocence and he was so sorry. Then he said he had been kidnapped as a little boy and molested badly. The Lord was healing him and He knew that the Lord wanted him to call me and ask my forgiveness. I was able to tell him that I had forgiven him years earlier.

One afternoon, I was ministering and praying for a man, and a demon surfaced. The demon was causing excruciating pain to his back and side. I could not make this demon stop or leave. I felt helpless. I pleaded the blood of *Yeshua* and told it to leave. I told it, I had power and authority to make it leave, however, nothing I said worked. After each command for it to leave, the demon would say arrogantly, "I am still here." This battle raged for two or three hours. I sensed the Holy Spirit directing me to ask the demon what gave it legal rights to be here. As I did, the demon spoke to me in a hideous laugh with great sarcasm, "I have this man's heart cut in four ways." The Lord told me this man was holding four people in un-forgiveness: his father, mother, sister and ex-wife. They had hurt him very badly emotionally. In the natural he had every right to hold them in un-forgiveness, for all that each of them had done to him. However, by not forgiving, it gave the demon a legal right to torment him.

I explained to the man that, because he was holding these people in unforgiveness, the demon had a right to be here. Through this knowledge, I was able to take him through a prayer to heal the hurt the four people had caused him and to release them from his un-forgiveness, anger, rage, and root of bitterness. The demon lost its power and the man was delivered. Praise God!

When Satan gets you into his prison, through emotional pain, he doesn't want to let you go. His time is short. We can't afford to hold onto unforgiveness. When we do, unforgiveness brings with it a spirit of torment. We see this in the Parable of the Unforgiving Servant.

Then Peter came to Him and said, "Lord, how often shall my brother sin against me, and I forgive him? Up to seven times?" Yeshua said to him, "I do not say to you, up to seven times, but up to seventy times seven. Therefore the kingdom of heaven is like a certain king who wanted to settle accounts with his servants. And when he had begun to settle accounts, one was brought to him who owed him ten thousand talents. But as he was not able to pay, his master commanded that he be sold, with his wife and children and all that he had, and that payment be made. The servant therefore fell down before him, saying, 'Master, have patience with me, and I will pay you all.' Then the master of that servant was moved with compassion, released him, and forgave him the debt. "But that servant went out and found one of his fellow servants who owed him a hundred denarii; and he laid hands on him and took him by the throat, saying, 'Pay me what you owe!' So his fellow servant fell down at his feet and begged him, saying, 'Have patience with me, and I will pay you all.' And he would not, but went and threw him into prison till he should pay the debt. So when his fellow servants saw what had been done, they were very grieved, and came and told their master all that had been done. Then his master, after he had called him, said to him, 'you wicked servant! I forgave you all that debt because you begged me. Should you not also have had compassion on your fellow servant, just as I had pity on you?' And his master was angry, and delivered him to the torturers until he should pay all that was due to him. "So My heavenly Father also will do to you if each of you, from his heart, does not forgive his brother his trespasses (Matthew 18:21-35).

Yeshua showed how unforgiveness could limit what God would do in others. (Note: the jailed fellow servant is still in prison in the story.) His master was angry, and delivered him to the torturers until he should pay all that was due to him. The torture, literally "bill collector," exacts its fee on our bodies, minds and emotions. If you have ever held anyone in unforgiveness or are holding them in unforgiveness you might have felt or you are feeling this torment. I have. When I would go to bed at night, I would lay there thinking about the person, and what they did or didn't do, what they said or didn't say. I would also think about what I would say or not say, arguing with them in my mind. I would wake up in the middle of the night, tossing and turning, thinking about the person. The first thing on my mind when I would wake up in the morning was that person, and I would start my day thinking about them all over again.

Yeshua shows us a different way of dealing with the wrong done to us, by extending his love and forgiveness. *Yeshua* became a sacrifice on the cross taking all the punishment we should have suffered for our sins. He has freely canceled the debt of all our wrongdoings. We too need to be able to extend that same grace to others.

It's like our Father is holding an IOU from us in his hand and we are holding an IOU of the people that we perceive have wronged us. God is saying if you tear up yours, I will tear up mine. *For if you forgive men when they sin against you, your heavenly Father will also forgive you. But if you do not forgive men their sins, your Father will not forgive your sins* (Matthew 6:14-15).

Get rid of all bitterness, rage and anger, brawling and slander, along with every form of malice. Be kind and compassionate to one another, forgiving each other, just as in Christ God (Elohim) forgave you (Ephesians 4:31-32).

You may say, "But you have never suffered like I have or been abused like I have." You may feel justified to feel hate, bitterness and anger towards that person or people that have hurt you.

Stuart Briscoe wrote, "Paul taught the Ephesian Christians that they were not to regard their struggles purely from a human point of view, but to recognize, *We do not wrestle against flesh and blood, but against principalities, against powers, against the rulers of the darkness of this age, against spiritual hosts of wickedness in the heavenly places"*(Ephesians 6:12). At the time, Paul was in prison at the mercy of the Emperor awaiting trial, which would eventually lead to his execution in Rome. So while he was struggling with the deprivations, indignities, discomforts and uncertainties of life in a Roman prison, he saw his struggle as more than that. It was not all about flesh and blood. He recognized he was involved in spiritual warfare.

Failure to recognize the reality of spiritual warfare by seeing the struggles of this life as nothing more than human struggles is as serious as a soldier on the battlefield failing to recognize the enemy and fighting the wrong battle. That would lead to defeat. We will do well to remember that as long as we inhabit a place in this world, we are living in a war zone. The forces of evil that are lined up against us are spiritual.[6]

Why Do We Find It So Hard to Forgive?

Forgiveness is difficult, because there is still hurt and pain attached to the unforgiveness. There could also be a spirit of offense. Satan uses offense to cause us to break fellowship with one another. This, in turn, causes resentment, anger, hatred, etc.

I have found that it is easier to forgive, if God heals the emotional pain first. Before trying to forgive, you should go to the Father in prayer. Ask Him to heal all the hurt and pain and remove the spirit of offense that is associated with the unforgiveness.

Sometimes we just have to give ourselves permission to forgive. This is a gift you give to yourself. Next, choose by your free will to let go of all bitterness, resentment, anger, rage and hatred.

At the beginning of my relationship with Benjamin, he would use his tongue to cut me. One time he had given me a tongue-lashing that was so hurtful; I told the Lord that was it. He could have this husband too. I grabbed my Bible as I went away to pray. I told the Lord He had better give me something because I was going to leave this relationship. I was severely wounded by Benjamins actions. Consequently, I was very angry. As I sat there praying, I opened up the Bible to Colossians 3.

In Colossians 3, Paul tells us, *If then you were raised with Christ, seek those things, which are above, where Christ is, sitting at the right hand of God. Set your mind on things above, not on things on the earth, for you died, and your life is hidden with Christ in God. When Christ who is our life appears, then you also will appear with Him in glory.... But now you yourselves are to put off all these: anger, wrath, malice, blasphemy, filthy language out of your mouth. ... and have put on the new man who is renewed in knowledge according to the image of Him who created him, ... Therefore, as the elect of God, holy and beloved,* **put on tender mercies, kindness, humility, meekness, long suffering;** *bearing with one another, and* **forgiving one another, if anyone has a complaint against another; even as Christ forgave you, so you also must do.** *But above all these things* **put on love,** *which is the bond of perfection. And let the peace of God rule in your hearts, to which also you were called in one body; and be thankful. ... And whatever you do in word or deed, do all in the name of the Lord Yeshua, giving thanks to God the Father through Him* (Colossians 3:1-4, 8, 10, 12-15, 17). (emphasis added)

As I was reading Colossians 3, all my anger dissipated. The thing that seemed so big was no longer very big. I had put my mind back on the things above and not below. Now I see that God used this time for my husband to see Christ in me. Also, my husband needed healing and deliverance. I was in a spiritual battle. I can see now why Satan wanted to wound me through my husband. He was afraid of what God was going to do with the two of us together. This ministry would not be where it is today, if it were not for Benjamin being in my life. The song "**Wind Beneath My Wings,**" sung by Bette Midler, describes very well, what my husband is to me. He is not only my Boaz, but he is the wind beneath my wings. If I had not read Colossians 3 and chosen to let go of the anger, bitterness and unforgiveness that day, I would hate to think where I would be today and how many blessings I would have missed.

If you are holding someone in unforgiveness and you are still very hurt over what they did or did not do, you may want to stop here and ask God to heal all the hurt that is behind the unforgiveness.

Forgiveness towards Others

It is absolutely essential to release feelings of bitterness and unforgiveness, in order to fully receive healing for our souls.

But he who hates his brother is in darkness and walks in darkness, and does not know where he is going, because the darkness has blinded his eyes (1 John 2:11).

But if you do not forgive men their trespasses, neither will your Father forgive your trespasses (Matthew 6:15).

And whenever you stand praying, if you have anything against anyone, forgive him, that your Father in heaven may also forgive you your trespasses. But if you do not forgive, neither will your Father in heaven forgive your trespasses (Mark 11:25-26).

Here is a prayer to help you release someone from unforgiveness

Father, I come to your throne room of grace... Thank you for your grace for me... I bring to you (name of person/persons), and I choose to release (person/persons) of all my anger, resentment, rage, hatred, bitterness and unforgiveness...I ask you to forgive, heal, deliver and bless (him/her). If he/she is not saved, send your Holy Spirit (*Ruach Hakodesh*) to them to woo them to You Father, and bring them into salvation. In *Yeshua's* name, Amen.

Forgiveness towards Self

There are times when we hold ourselves in unforgiveness and we need to forgive ourselves. After I had been walking with the Lord for quite some time, temptation came in. I could feel the power of God protecting me. It was as though He was standing between me and the temptation. I told the Lord to move out of my way. I wanted the sin. I could literally feel God move out of my way and I went for the sin. I fell hard. At first, the sin was very exciting. But, as always, sin costs more than you want to pay. Sin takes you further than you want to go. At the end of this sin, I saw a vision of myself laying in the gutter. My clothes were ripped and dirty. Satan was standing over me kicking me in the ribs saying, "You thought that sin was for your pleasure. It was for your destruction." I was overcome with guilt, shame and regret. I did not want to pray. I did not want God to even look at me. The Holy Spirit was tugging at me to pray, but I kept pushing Him away. I couldn't forgive myself. I knew I had deliberately sinned.

When I first came to the Lord, and he had me repent of the sins I had committed before I was saved, it was easy to receive forgiveness. Even as I was growing in the things of God, He would correct me, and show me sin that I committed in ignorance. I would repent and turn from it and be cleansed. I could receive forgiveness for those sins.

I had tasted the goodness of the Lord, and I was filled with the Holy Spirit, however, I had blatantly sinned. I told the Lord, "I cannot receive YOUR forgiveness this time. It's different Lord, I know better." I felt I had gotten so far away from God that I couldn't go back to Him. The Lord told me that the blood of *Yeshua* is for our past, present and future sins. When Satan traps us, we need to repent and run back to the Father. When we don't forgive ourselves we are saying the blood of *Yeshua* is not good enough to blot out our sin.

The story of the Prodigal Son, (By Mary Fairchild)

"*Yeshua* tells the story of a man who has two sons. The younger son asks his father to give him his portion of the family estate as an early inheritance. Once received, the son promptly sets off on a long journey to a distant land and begins to waste his fortune on wild living. When the money runs out, a severe famine hits the country and the son finds himself in dire circumstances. He takes a job feeding pigs. He is so destitute that he even longs to eat the food assigned to the pigs.

The young man finally comes to his senses, remembering his father. In humility, he recognizes his foolishness, decides to return to his father and ask for forgiveness and mercy. The father who had been watching and waiting, receives his son back with open arms of compassion. He is overjoyed by the return of his lost son! Immediately the father turns to his servants and asks them to prepare a giant feast in celebration.

Typically, a son would receive his inheritance at the time of his father's death. The fact that the younger brother instigated the early division of the family estate showed a rebellious and proud disregard for his father's authority, not to mention a selfish and immature attitude.

Pigs are unclean animals. Jews were not even allowed to touch pigs. When the son took a job feeding pigs, even longing for their food to fill his belly, it reveals that he had fallen as low as he could possibly go."[7]

I could relate to this son. I was living in rebellion to God. Sometimes we have to hit rock bottom before we come to our senses and recognize our sin.

In this story, the father is a picture of the Heavenly Father. God waits patiently, with loving compassion to restore us, if we return to him with humble hearts. He offers us everything in his kingdom, restoring full relationship with joyful celebration. He doesn't even dwell on our past waywardness. As we read, *As far as the east is from the west, so far has He removed our transgressions from us* (Psalm 103:12). We also read, *How much more shall the blood of Christ, who through the eternal Spirit offered Himself without spot to God, cleanse your conscience from dead works to serve the living God?* (Hebrews 9:14)

Prayer to help you release yourself of unforgiveness

Father, I repent of all my known and unknown sins. Father, your word says if I confess my sin...You are faithful to forgive me... Your word says that the blood of *Yeshua* was shed for me... for my past, present and future sins. I now receive that forgiveness, and I release myself from all unforgiveness, in *Yeshua's* name, Amen.

Forgiveness towards God

Sometimes we blame God for the things that have hurt us. Consciously or unconsciously, we think all of these things are God's fault. We have deep-seated resentment. We cannot have resentment toward God and experience kingdom power flowing in our lives. We have to rid ourselves of any bitterness toward God.

Prayer to release God of unforgiveness

Father, I release you from all of my anger, rage, and resentment... I know now that all things work together for good, and you will not give me more than I can handle. You will always help me carry the load. Please forgive me for holding you in unforgiveness. I love you, in *Yeshua's* name, Amen

Chapter 10

Deliverance from Generational Curses

—◦◦◦◦—

" *A* generational curse is basically a defilement that was passed down from one generation to another. For example, if your mother has been heavily involved in the occult, then she has become quite defiled (polluted or unclean), and has opened herself up to allow demons to enter her. The Bible tells us that the sin of the parents can cause that same pollution to be handed down to their children:

*Our fathers have sinned, and are not; and we have borne their iniquities (*Lamentations 5:7).

You shall not bow down to them nor serve them. For I, the Lord your God, am a jealous God, visiting the iniquity of the fathers upon the children to the third and fourth generations of those who hate Me (Exodus 20:5).

Not only is the uncleanliness handed down, but the demons can also move in and take advantage of this. This can happen at a very young age in a person's life (often before birth). The person then goes throughout life struggling with the same bondage that their parents struggle with."[8]

I had generational curses from my parents. I did not know I was in battle with demons. My parents were alcoholics. My mother was a drug user. Both had a spirit of lust and seduction. I wrestled with alcohol, drugs and sexual sins. Through revelation knowledge, the Lord showed me that I had opened a door for the demons to control the next generation through these sins. I saw that these same demons had legal rights over my children. Thankfully, the Lord delivered me of these demons.

If you struggle with the same bondages as your parents, or see siblings with the same problems, then it is quite possible that you are suffering from the effects of a generational curse. Many times, when you see three generations suffering from depression it is almost always a generational curse at work. Spirits of heaviness can take advantage of those curses through the defilement passed down through the generations.

Not everything is a demon. I believe dysfunction can be passed down. As an example, as a child, our family moved many times. Then, as an adult, I moved many times with my daughter Pamela.

One day a woman brought her five-year-old boy to my office. This little boy was bouncing off the walls. He could not be still for a moment. I asked the mother what was going on with her son. She said that his voice would change and he would threaten to kill her. He would get so out of hand, that her father, whom she lived with, would have to step in and stop him from hurting her. She said she feared for her life. I felt this was passed down from generations. I felt the Holy Spirit wanted me to ask if anyone in her family was into Freemasonry, and she said, "Yes." Her grandfather and father were both thirty-three degree masons. Her father cleaned the lodge and was always there. He would take the little boy with him when he went. I have seen generational curses on people whose bloodline had been in the Freemasons. She wanted me to preform deliverance. I could not get her to understand that it was her bloodline that opened up the doors for the demons. She would have to repent of her father and grandfather's sins and renounce them. I also felt she needed to leave her father's house. Her father could no longer take her son to the lodge. She was unwilling to do any of these things. She brought the boy back a couple of years later. He was worse. I still could not set him free because of the legal rights the demons had over him and his bloodline.

Freemasons have mixed idolatry, paganism, the occult, Gnosticism, Kabbala, fertility cults, Satanism, spiritualism, and demonology. To find out more on Freemasonry, go to http://www.bibleprobe.com/freemasonry.htm

The good news is you can be set free and completely released from the effects of any generational curses handed down to you. The Blood of *Yeshua* is more powerful than any bondage that may have been handed down to you!

I believe generational sin curses (curses caused by sins of the forefathers) are automatically broken at the time a person receives salvation, but the unclean spirits that entered in before they accepted *Yeshua* still need to come out. Other generational curses, such as those encountered through Freemasonry, need to be renounced and broken in order to be set free from them. Once a curse is broken, the next step is to drive out the spirits that may have entered in because of that curse.

Prayer to break generational curses:

Father, I confess all my known and unknown sins and known and unknown sins of my parents (name specific sins if known), grandparents (name specific sins if known), and all other ancestors all the way back to Adam. In the name of *Yeshua*, and by the power of His blood, I now renounce, break and sever all cords of iniquity and generational curses I have inherited from my parents, grandparents and all other ancestors. I break and sever all taproots, unholy soul ties and any ancestral vows and seals. In the name of *Yeshua*, I now loose myself and my future generations from any bondage passed down to me from my ancestors. I command any evil spirits, which have taken advantage of these cords of iniquity, generational curses and unholy soul ties to leave me and go directly to the abyss now, in the name of *Yeshua*!

It is also important to remember that God shows mercy to a thousand generation to those who keep His commandments. *... but showing mercy to thousands, to those who love Me and keep My commandments* (Exodus 20:6).

Curses

The Bible speaks of the tremendous power of words, both for good and evil, for blessing and cursing. God spoke creation into existence. His words have ultimate power and authority. Since we are created in the image of God, it stands to reason that our words also carry power. *Death and life are in the power of the tongue and those who love it will eat its fruit* (Proverbs 18:21).

It is true: words can bring life or death, healing or hurt, blessing, or cursing. We read, *But no man can tame the tongue. It is an unruly evil, full of deadly poison. With it we bless our God and Father, and with it we curse men, who have been made in the similitude of God. Out of the same mouth proceed blessing and cursing. My brethren, these things ought not to be so* (James 3:8-10).

Just as we can speak in such a way that blesses people and builds them up, we can also speak curses over people's lives. A curse is a supernatural force to bring harm and destruction to a person's life. Curses may be manifest in various ways. Be sure that this is not some superstitious or primitive belief. The Bible speaks about blessings and curses. These are both real forces in the world.

There was a word curse on my life growing up. My nickname was dumb-dumb. By the time I was eighteen, I truly thought of myself as stupid - not able to learn anything. Why should I even try? I was trying to survive my childhood, so I had a very hard time staying focused in school. This validated the curse. When I started painting, the Lord showed me the curse that had been put on me in my childhood and how I believed it. He then broke the curse off of me.

Word curses are real. Let us look at Balaam's attempts to curse Israel. *Therefore please come at once, curse this people for me, for they are too mighty for me. Perhaps I shall be able to defeat them and drive them out of the land, for I know that he whom you bless is blessed, and he whom you curse is cursed* (Numbers 22:6).

Joshua cursed whoever rebuilt Jericho. *Then Joshua charged them at that time, saying, 'Cursed be the man before the LORD (Yahweh) who rises up and builds this city Jericho; he shall lay its foundation with his firstborn, and with his youngest he shall set up its gate* (Joshua 6:26).

This curse was fulfilled; *In his days Hiel of Bethel built Jericho. He laid its foundation with Abiram his firstborn, and with his youngest son Segub he set up its gates, according to the word of the LORD, which He had spoken through Joshua the son of Nun* (I Kings 16:34). This curse manifested itself over five hundred years later as Abiram and Segub, the sons of Hiel of Bethel, died.

Prayer:

Father, I break all word curses over my life. I repent of any and all word curses that I have spoken over myself or anyone else. Now I ask that you would replace these word curses with a blessing, in Yeshua's name, Amen.

Chapter 11

Breaking Soul Ties
& Removing What Is Accursed

———⁎———

The Bible speaks of what is today known as soul ties. In the Bible, it doesn't use the word soul tie, but it speaks of a soul tie when it talks about souls being knit together, becoming one flesh. *For this cause shall a man leave his father and mother, and shall be joined unto his wife, and they two shall be one flesh* (Ephesians 5:31). We see that David and Jonathan had a soul tie: *Now when he had finished speaking to Saul, the soul of Jonathan was knit to the soul of David, and Jonathan loved him as his own soul* (I Samuel 18:1). A soul tie is an emotional bond or connection that unites you with someone else.

You can become bound to a person through your soul. This tie is formed through: close friendships, vows, commitments, promises, and physical intimacy.

A soul tie can serve many functions, but in its simplest form, it ties two souls together in the spiritual realm.

How Soul Ties Are Formed

A soul tie binds our thought, emotions and will to another person. We think about them. They have won our hearts. We will to have them in our lives. In the demonic world, unholy soul ties can give demons legal rights to travel back and forth from one person to the other. Here are some ways that unhealthy soul ties are formed:

- Abusive relationships (physical, sexual, emotional, verbal)
- Adulterous affairs
- Sex before marriage
- Obsessive entanglements with a person (giving them more authority in your life than you give to God)
- Controlling relationships

Godly soul ties are formed when a couple is married. "The two," He says, "shall become one flesh" (Genesis 2:24). However, when a person has ungodly sexual relations with another person, an ungodly soul tie is then formed. *Or do you not know that he who is joined to a harlot is one body with her?* (I Corinthians 6:16a). Unholy soul ties can also be formed from relationships that are nonsexual in nature, by being tied to anyone that is ungodly. [8]

When I went to Cancun, Mexico, to minister, I met a woman that had all of the above. Her mother, who had passed away, had been involved in a cult and had been an abusive mother. When I met this young woman she was a single mother of two. She wanted to receive *Yeshua* as her personal savior. I lead her through a sinner's prayer. As soon as I did, demons surfaced. She told me that as soon as her mother died she started feeling like her mother. For instance, when she walked down the stairs she did not feel like herself any longer. She said her body language became like her mother's. She also became abusive to her children, as her mother was to her and her siblings. After her mother's death, her father started dating a young woman about the same age as she was. This woman was into witchcraft.

When the Lord started delivering this woman, nothing was going to stop it. I had never encountered someone that had so many demons. One demon after another would come to the surface. This went on for hours. The best description of this activity is to compare it to the birthing of a baby. Once the baby starts exiting the womb, nothing will stop it. In the same manner the demons were surfacing. The Lord was gracious as He gave us discernment. The demons had entered her when her mother died because of the soul tie she had to her. Then the woman her father had been dating wanted all of the grown children out of the way. She began putting witchcraft curses on his children to kill them. On a return ministry trip to Cancun, a couple of months later, I had the privilege of seeing this woman. She was a changed woman. She had become a loving mother to her children. It was a very great difference. The Lord told me, "Look at the fruit of your labor. Generations have been changed." Praise the LORD!

How to break a soul tie

1. If any sins were committed to cause this soul tie, repent of them! Fornication is perhaps one of the most common ways to create unholy soul ties.
2. Gifts given to you by the other person in connection with the sin or unholy relationship, such as rings, cards, pictures, etc. Such things symbolize the ungodly relationship, and can hold a soul tie in place. You should get rid of them!
3. Any rash vows or commitments made that played a part in forming the soul tie should be renounced and repented of, and broken in *Yeshua*'s name Even things like "I will love you forever," or "I could never love another person like I love you," need to be renounced. They are spoken commitments that need to be undone verbally. As Proverbs 21:23 tells us, "Whoever guards his mouth and tongue keeps his soul from troubles." The tongue has the ability to bring the soul great troubles and bondage.
4. Forgive that person if you have anything against them.
5. Renounce the soul tie. Do this verbally, and in *Yeshua's* name. Example, "In *Yeshua's* name, I now renounce any ungodly soul ties formed between myself and _____ as a result of _____ (fornication, any sin, etc.)."
6. Break the soul tie in *Yeshua's* name! Do this verbally using your authority in *Yeshua*. Example, "I now break and sever any ungodly soul ties formed between myself and _____ as a result of _____ (fornication, etc.) in *Yeshua*' name."[8]

Accursed Things

A woman brought her six-year-old daughter to me because her daughter had become very fearful. To say the child had become fearful is an understatement. She was terrified. She wouldn't sleep in her bed any longer. Every night she had to be with her mother. Her Father was upset that she wouldn't sleep in her own bed. I asked the mother a few questions, "When did this start? Had something changed in your life when this started?" The Mother replied, "Yes, My sister-in-law passed away two years ago. When she died my brother-in-law asked if we wanted some of her things. I said, 'Yes.' My sister-in-law had a lot of things when she died. When she needed something, instead of buying one item, she would buy twelve or more. So I have a lot of her possessions."

One morning, around two or three, she said that her husband was using the restroom and he heard an audible voice say, "Leave my stuff alone." I then asked her if her sister-in-law had been a nice woman. She said, "NO, she was into witchcraft." The Lord revealed that she had an accursed thing in her house. *And you, by all means abstain from the accursed things, lest you become accursed when you take of the accursed things, and make the camp of Israel a curse, and trouble it* (Joshua 6:18). Achan, alone, defied the ban. His disobedience impacted the whole nation of Israel. This is due to an Old Testament inferred principle of corporate solidarity.

But the children of Israel committed a trespass regarding the accursed things, for Achan the son of Carmi, the son of Zabdi, the son of Zerah, of the tribe of Judah, took of the accursed things; so the anger of the LORD (Yahweh) burned against the children of Israel (Joshua 7:1).

Therefore the children of Israel could not stand before their enemies, but turned their backs before their enemies, because they have become doomed to destruction. Neither will I be with you anymore, unless you destroy the accursed from among you. Get up, sanctify the people, and say, 'sanctify yourselves for tomorrow, because thus says the LORD (Yahweh) God (Elohim) of Israel: 'There is an accursed thing in your midst, O Israel; you cannot stand before your enemies until you take away the accursed thing from among you (Joshua 7:12-13).

So Joshua sent messengers, and they ran to the tent; and there it was, hidden in his tent, with the silver under it. And they took them from the midst of the tent, brought them to Joshua and to all the children of Israel, and laid them out before the LORD (Yahweh)." Then Joshua, and all Israel with him, took Achan the son of Zerah, the silver, the garment, the wedge of gold, his sons, his daughters, his oxen, his donkeys, his sheep, his tent, and all that he had, and they brought them to the Valley of Achor. And Joshua said, "Why

have you troubled us? The LORD (Yahweh) will trouble you this day."
So all Israel stoned him with stones; and they burned them with fire
after they had stoned them with stones (Joshua 7:22-25).

The whole nation could not stand against their enemy. Achan's family was destroyed because of the principle of corporate guilt that is similar to the corporate solidarity mentioned above. This is symbolic of how the enemy can destroy our families today. As noted above, it only took one person to bring destruction to the entire bloodline; the sins of our forefathers' impact future generations.

We are all aware that Satan and his demons are our enemies. We know that they war against true believers, churches, and other Christian institutions. Most of us can quote verbatim parts of Ephesians 6:10-20, James 4:7-8, 1 Peter 5:8-11, and other spiritual warfare passages. The question is, do we really comprehend the power hurled against us by Satan and his demons? Do we really know what Satan can do in the lives of believers who violate God's Word, even through ignorance?

People allow the enemy legal rights to their home because of items they have brought in either before or after salvation. These items include such things as: drugs, idols, crystals used in the new age movement, some (not all) inherited items passed down for generations or from deceased relatives (that the enemy could have a legal right to), witchcraft books, anything to do with the occult (some people at Halloween decorate their houses with all sorts of witchcraft and evil, if they only knew how Halloween is the highest satanic day on the calendar they would want nothing to do with it), horoscopes, pornography, and evil games such as dungeons and dragons, and games and movies that promote murder, (one young man said he watched movies about murder then he would fantasize that he was killing people, he would walk around at night with a knife thinking about how he would kill someone), etc.

I encourage you to ask the Lord if there is any accursed thing in your home that you need to get rid of. Ask Him to expose everything. If the Lord shows you anything, ask the Lord what you should do with it. He might have you pray over it and cover it with the blood of *Yeshua* or it might need to be thrown away or burned.

When I was a young Christian, right after I had received the baptism of the Holy Spirit, I started having nightmares. In these dreams I was being chased. This same dream recurred for several nights. The last night I had it, the being that was chasing me caught up to me, grabbed me, and as I turned around to face him, I saw it was Satan. He told me that if I gave him my soul he would give me the power I was longing for. When he said that, fear overwhelmed me. I was shaken. I screamed at him, "No, I am a Christian!" The next day, I told a mature believer my dream. She asked if I had any witchcraft books in my house. I said, "YES, I do not know how it got in my house. I keep wanting to read it, but I have not." She told me to burn it in my fireplace. I did as she suggested. Fear filled my home, however, the Lord told me He was with me.

The Ephesian believers set an example in dealing with occult items. They confessed their involvement with such as sin and burned the items publicly *This became known both to all Jews and Greeks dwelling in Ephesus; and fear fell on them all, and the name of the Lord Jesus was magnified. And many who had believed came confessing and telling their deeds. Also, many of those who had practiced magic brought their books together and burned them in the sight of all. And they counted up the value of them, and it totaled fifty thousand pieces of silver* (Acts 19:17-19).

The first step in dealing with accursed things is to pray, asking the Lord to show you the accursed item (s) and to tell you what to do. You must obey. The second step is to pray over your home and command any demon that was let in, to leave in the name of *Yeshua* of Nazareth.

The third step is to ask for the Holy Spirit to come and fill your home with His presence.

Chapter 12

Cancelling Satan's Special Assignments & Attacks

---

*S*atan sends special assignments. When he knows you have an assignment from the Lord to accomplish a mandate, he sends demons to attack and stop you.

For we do not wrestle against flesh and blood, but against principalities, against powers, against the rulers of the darkness of this age, against spiritual hosts of wickedness in the heavenly places (Ephesians 6:12).

In 2014, half of our core group at the ministry ended up leaving. Our core group was strong. They loved the ministry, and they were dedicated to the anointing. They gave their time and resources. They were strong pillars. They had all been personally touched and had experienced miracles in their lives by this anointing. However, half of this group came to me with some complaints. There was a spirit of offense on them that turned into a root of bitterness. Soon these people left.

We were all shocked - especially the other half of the core group. We could not believe that these people, of all people, would leave the ministry.

One woman from this group kept coming, however, you could see on her a spirit of heaviness as if she could barely drag herself into church. She asked to meet with me. She was so depressed and burdened. In the meeting she shared with me how she felt after the other ones left. She felt that everyone at church was rejecting her and that I did not love her, even though every time she came to church I would hug her and tell her how much I loved her. She said she heard me say the words, but every sermon I preached, she thought, was directed at her to wound and hurt her. This was not the case at all. She would leave church more depressed. As we started praying, a demon surfaced. I asked, "What gave you a legal right to be here," and it said that it was an assignment.

I then asked, "What was the assignment?" It said, "Destruction, to destroy her." There were several demons that night that manifested: rejection, sadness, and depression to name a few. These demons wanted her and the others out of the ministry. We got victory that night. She did not leave the ministry, and the Lord is using this woman mightily.

The Lord prayed for Peter's faith not to fail him. Then he told Peter, "Strengthen your brother."

And the Lord said, "Simon, Simon! Indeed, Satan has asked for you, that he may sift you as wheat. But I have prayed for you, that your faith should not fail; and when you have returned to Me, strengthen your brethren" (Luke 22:31-32).

How important it is to have faith when we are going through such a trial. We also have to be sober and vigilant in our walk. This woman at church was resisting as much as she knew how. Her vigilance paid off when she was delivered.

Be sober, be vigilant; because your adversary the devil walks about like a roaring lion, seeking whom he may devour. Resist him, steadfast in the faith, knowing that the same sufferings are experienced by your brotherhood in the world. But may the God of all grace, who called us to His eternal glory by Christ Jesus, after you have suffered a while, perfect, establish, strengthen, and settle you (1 Peter 5:8-10).

These demonic assignments can be against other areas in our lives such as our homes, families and jobs etc. Remember, demons are there to try and stop what God has for us.

Canceling Assignments

Prayer:

Father, I acknowledge that You are the ruler far above all principalities, powers and dominions. In the Name of *Yeshua,* I break all assignments set against me. In *Yeshua's* name, I ask that You would cancel any such assignment and prevent all influences by forces of darkness. To all evil spirits and forces of darkness allowed access through this assignment, I renounce Satan and all his works and all his ways and send all of you to the abyss, in the Name of *Yeshua.* Amen.

Inner Vows

An inner vow is self-determination, set by the mind and heart, into a person's being, early in life. Vows we make currently also affect us, but an inner vow is a promise we make to ourselves as children, and is usually forgotten. Our inner being persistently retains such programming no matter what changes of mind and heart may later pertain. The distinctive mark of an inner vow is it resists the normal maturation process. Inner vows resist change. We do not grow out of them.

An inner vow is as if you are telling yourself the way things are going to be. Some examples are:

"I will never do that again."

"I will never be like my mother."

"I will never allow that in my house."

We are telling ourselves how reality is going to be. Truthfully, that is not necessarily God's will for our lives.

The inner vows that are made in childhood, and that we have forgotten, seem to be even more powerful than the ones we've made as adults – even to the point where they can affect growth and development. Words have more than psychological power. They also have spiritual power. When we made those vows, our enemy, the devil, worked hard to make those negative words come true. [8]

I prayed for a woman who had a manifested demon whose legal right existed because of an inner vow. Her father was verbally abusive and would always tell her she was never going to amount to anything. She was no good. She would go into her bedroom and say over and over, "I will amount to something, I will do well and I will be someone." When the demon surfaced it told her if she made it leave then she would be what her father said about her, because it had given her the strength to do what she has done. She was a very successful businesswoman and she was afraid if the demon left her she would be nothing and lose everything that she had built. She had built walls up around her heart, which caused her to have a stony heart. She also had a lot of pride in what "she had made of herself." When we broke the inner vow the LORD (*Yahweh*) was able to bring deliverance to her.

Inner vows may not become manifest immediately in behavior. They may rest totally forgotten and dormant, until triggered by the right person or situation. Having forgotten them, we are unaware that they exist or that they could have any effect on our relationships or us. They are often difficult to identify and take on a life of their own within us. This causes us to deal with reality in a particular way.

Scriptural basis for the "inner vow" For *as he thinks in his heart, so is he* (Proverbs 23:7).

- We first have to identify the vow we have made. Sometimes we do not even think about inner vows we made so long ago. We need our heavenly Father to reveal them to us. We can do this by asking Him to show us if we have made an inner vow. Then we need to renounce the vow we have made.

- Prayer to break an inner vow:
Father, I confess and renounce the inner vow _____. In *Yeshua*'s name I break the bondage of this vow. Heal the area in my heart that caused me to make this vow. By the blood of *Yeshua*, I declare and decree that I am free from this vow and that I am free to be who You intended me to be. Amen!

- Finally, ask *Yeshua* to provide the freedom from the vow and to reveal the newness of your life in Him, regarding your destiny and true identity. [8]

Chapter 13

Birthing of the Anointing

My little children, of whom I travail in birth again until
Christ be formed in you
(Galatians 4:19).

I got my husband off to work and my children to school. I could not wait to get settled down in my rocking chair to pray as I did most mornings. However, this morning was different. After praising the Lord for a few minutes and thanking Him for his great love, I could feel his Holy Spirit. He always feels sweet, however heavy. As I sat before Him, I could feel His presence get stronger and stronger. As I was enjoying His presence and the great peace He brings, something very different happened to me. It is very hard to describe, but I will try. I started feeling like I was giving birth. I was not pregnant and this was not physical. My breathing increased. I became very warm. My body was shaking with His power. I knew something spiritual was happening, however, I did not know what. I had never had anything like this happen to me before. I was not frightened because there still was a strong feeling of His presence and intense peace upon me.

After it seemed to lift, I asked the Lord, "What just happened?" He said, "You just gave birth to the anointing that is on your life." It was a spiritual birth not a physical one. I questioned the Lord, "What do you mean, I just gave birth to the anointing?" I was confused. I did not understand what He meant. The Holy Spirit had been moving through my life. I had seen many miracles; healing, deliverance and people being set free. So I asked, "Father, if I just now gave birth to the anointing, what have I been doing in the spiritual realm up to now? People have been healed and delivered. I have witnessed your great power so many times and I have seen many miracles. I do not understand." The Lord said, "You have been pregnant and in labor with the anointing, now you have given birth to it. It is now outside of you and will have a life of its own. It will continue to grow. Just like you look at your natural children and see how they have grown, so will it be with this anointing ."

I had been ministering inner healing and deliverance, on a regular basis, to about twenty women. It started out with selling Jafra, a woman's skin care line. I was at the home of a woman from church, to teach a makeup class. In the middle of my sales pitch, one woman asked, "Aren't you the Amen Lady?" (This was the name my pastor gave me, because I was always yelling amen, when I would get excited about something he was saying.) I said, "Yes." That day, I went from selling Jafra to these women to ministering to them. I do not think I sold anything that day. I started praying for the women and the power and glory showed up. These women were being healed and delivered. They asked if we could get together once a month (not for skin care) for the care of the soul. I agreed. After several months of ministering to them, they wanted to be taught to do the same so that they could bring healing to others.

As I prayed about this matter, the Lord gave me the outline for, Boot Camp Basic Training. This is a ten-session teaching series that equips the believers by preparing them for their destiny, call and purpose, and by teaching them how to bring about healing and deliverance.

Geneva, one of the women that had been healed and delivered, told her Pastor about the ministry and how it had healed her. The pastor wanted to meet with me. I met with Pastor Mary. She asked if I would teach Boot Camp Basic Training at her church. I agreed to come and teach it. I sent out invitations to advertise the ten-week teaching, I put my name and home address as the return information on the envelope. The Lord said to put the ministry's name *Without Spot or Wrinkle Ministries International* on it instead of mine. Two days later, someone sent a check for a hundred dollars made out to the ministry. I did not know how to handle this check. We were not established yet as a ministry.

Pastor Mary taught me how to open up a ministry bank account. With a ministry account I had to register the ministry as doing business. On the way to the San Bernardino County Recorder-Clerk, where marriages and births are recorded, I strongly felt the presence of God. He spoke and said, "You are not recording a business. You are recording the birth of the anointing."

Moving the Ministry Out of Our Home

Just as the Lord had said the anointing started growing. As it grew, we grew out of our home. It started taking over our lives. The phone would start ringing at 6:30 a.m. and it would continue until 11:30 p.m. People were coming from everywhere. My husband felt it best that I not counsel and do deliverance in our home any longer. My children were being affected by it and we had no real family time.

We met some friends, Sue and Dave (not their real names) through another ministry where we were involved. Their marriage had been healed through this anointing and they loved what God (*Elohim*) was doing. As the ministry started to grow we invited them to be part of the ministry.

We started praying about moving the ministry out of our home. There was a lot to take into consideration. Should we start a non-profit? How do you start a non-profit? Benjamin, Sue and I met with an adviser to learn how to become a non-profit organization. Instead of encouragement, the adviser discouraged us by telling us how hard it would be to become a non-profit ministry. There would be a lot of paper work. It would be very expensive to obtain an attorney and file the necessary papers. There would be a business side to the ministry and we would have to keep great financial records. When the adviser left I started to cry. I felt so overwhelmed. I knew the ministry was growing and we had to move it out of our home. We were now going to have to go to a whole new level. It would be too hard. The LORD (*Yahweh*) was moving through me to heal people and set them free from demons. However, I did not want to take on the IRS.

Sue said, "I hate to say this, because I know we should never go into business with family or friends. Saying that, I can do the business side. Before I quit my job to stay home with my girls, I worked for a company that did payroll. I did the payroll." So with her help we opened up our first office in Covina, California. We became a non-profit Para-church ministry. The LORD (*Yahweh*) said the name was Without Spot or Wrinkle Ministries International. Sue thought "International" was too much so she left it off of the name, when she was filing the paperwork.

Our first office space was two upstairs rooms about 196 total square feet. The rent was four hundred eighty dollars a month. This was a stretch of faith, because the ministry had no credit. My husband was going to have to be responsible for the finances. This was a time that finances were very tight. My husband was working hard to keep me at home with our children. Now we were taking on an unbudgeted debt. My husband thought, at first, we would be able to charge people to come and be ministered to. However, the Lord said, "No, freely you have received, freely give." We had to trust the Lord that he would provide. He did.

The attorney we hired told us it would cost five hundred dollars to file the paperwork. This was money we did not have. However, we went forward in faith. One morning on my way in to the office, I had to make three stops. At each stop, someone put money in my hand and said the Lord told me to give you this money. The total amount came to twelve hundred dollars. When I arrived at the office, Sue looked like she saw a ghost. She said, "I just hung up from the attorney and he said it was twelve hundred dollars, not five hundred dollars. He did not know how I misunderstood him." I opened my hand and there was the twelve hundred dollars.

Vision of a Tidal Wave

When we opened the office it was such hard work. We had nothing. We needed phones, desks, chairs, etc. One day, when I arrived at home, out of sheer exhaustion, I threw myself across my bed to get a short nap before I picked up my children from school. As I was lying there, I started to pray in the spirit. (When I received the baptism of the Holy Spirit, He gave me the gift called speaking in tongues. This is how I pray in the spirit.) The Lord gave me a vision of a Tidal Wave. This Tidal Wave was at least fifty feet tall. It was standing straight up, stalled in midair. I saw myself at the office building, boarding up the windows, as someone would do to prepare for a hurricane. I was getting ready for this great Tidal Wave to hit. The Lord said, "The Tidal Wave represents the Holy Spirit. There is going to be a great outpouring of My Spirit like no one has ever seen before, and you are in preparation for this outpouring."

Six months later, He showed me another vision of the Tidal Wave. This time I saw myself standing on the beach. I was knee deep in fish. As far as my eye could see there were fish everywhere. The Tidal Wave had come in, and had receded back out to sea. Then the Lord said, "The Tidal Wave represents the outpouring of My Spirit and the fish represent the people that are going to come in due to this outpouring. However, the fish will need to be cleaned. If they stay out in the hot sun they will become very stinky and rotten."

I felt overwhelmed. There are many people that are going to need to be healed emotionally and delivered, due to the spiritual darkness that is

91

over the whole earth and the people. However, the Lord is going to pour out His Spirit.

Arise, shine; For your light has come! And the glory of the Lord is risen upon you. For behold, the darkness shall cover the earth, and deep darkness the people; but the Lord will arise over you, and His glory will be seen upon you. The Gentiles shall come to your light, and kings to the brightness of your rising. "Lift up your eyes all around, and see: They all gather together, they come to you. (Isaiah 60:1-4)

One of the many miracles we saw at this building

A young man attended a Boot Camp Basic Training that I was teaching. After the ten-week series I scheduled a one-on-one appointment with him in my office. In his appointment he told me he had gotten into heavy drug use and sin. Demons had overtaken him. He felt like he had lost his mind. No medical doctor could help him. One day, in his bedroom, his mom started praying for him. The demons surfaced and started speaking to her. She was very frightened. She did not know what to do. She called TBN. The prayer partner who answered her call knew of our ministry and told her about it and about the teaching of Boot Camp God (*Elohim*) restored his mind and he was healed completely.

His mother was so blessed that the Lord restored her son's mind she decided she wanted to come in for an appointment. She is about four feet, eleven inches tall. I remember thinking how easy this session was going to be. I had gotten to know her as I ministered to her son. She seemed so sweet. She was sweet, but the demons had a strong hold on her because of all the hurt of her past. There was a great manifestation of a demon of murder on her. That demon wanted to take her out of my office and down to the parking lot, so it could kill her. It said it could not kill her in my office. The demon had legal rights to her due to word curses of murder, through abuse that she had suffered growing up. However, on that day she was healed and delivered. Today she has a Spanish-speaking ministry setting people free.

Through this time Sue was amazing. There was not anything she could not do. My husband was so busy working that he was not at the office much, in those days. I started to trust and rely on Sue for everything. Everything that needed to be done around the ministry, she said she could do. She helped get office furniture, our first computer, answered phones, scheduled all my appointments and took care of all of the finances.

We were starting to grow out of the office. We found out the owner sold the building, and the new owners wanted to increase our rent. The season for this office was up. It was time we looked for another one. I know the Lord had to do it this way, because I often want to stay in a season longer than I should, even though that season is over. The Lord had to push me out.

It was time to start looking for our next office building. We looked and looked. It was not an easy task to find a building for a ministry. There was always a parking issue. Cities have a lot of rules and regulations for non-profits regarding what they can and cannot do. We finally found our next building. It was in a strip mall. The space had been a pizza restaurant that had gone out of business when a movie theater, the anchor store, went out of business. This building was 2600 square feet. It seemed so big compared to the first office. We turned the kitchen into four offices for counseling. Again, my husband and I were stretched in faith. Believing that God had met all of our needs at the first office, we knew He could meet them at this new building. The rent in this new building had more than tripled from what we were paying at the old office.

Godly Counsel?

*Where no counsel is, the people fall: but in the **multitude** of counselors there is safety* (Proverbs 11:14).

I was already counseling almost every day and teaching Boot Camp Basic Training. Along with emotional healing and deliverance, I was seeing physical healings as well. I got some "Godly" people together, along with our board members, to talk about the plans for this new building. In this meeting, we discussed what programs or teachings we could put in place. I had wanted to have a miracle healing service on Friday nights and see the Holy Spirit move in a powerful way; I wanted signs and wonders as in the New Testament days.

Good Ideas

During this meeting, one of the women reached over and put her hand on my knee and gave me a pat. She said, "You don't want to get too spiritual. After all, people need to have fun."

We had recently had a birthday party for Dave where there was a karaoke machine. We had so much fun. So we decided on Friday nights, instead of a miracle service, we would have praise and worship followed by karaoke. Additionally, it was decided that we would have Monday night Football for the men, during the football season. These all sounded like good ideas.

On the night of karaoke the people started complaining they had just come from church and did not want to sit through more praise and worship. So, we removed praise and worship and gave the people what they wanted. On top of that, the songs people chose to sing for karaoke reminded others of emotional hurt and pain from past failed relationships. On more than one occasion, someone left crying, because a certain song brought back so many memories. It then went from karaoke, to bringing in "Christian bands." It was Dave's dream to have a Christian nightclub, promoting Christian bands. He had promoted worldly bands and he was a natural at it.

When Dave was growing up, his family had a little sandwich shop and he wanted to open something like that again. When this building was a restaurant, it had a bar. We ended up turning this into a coffee bar, and started serving food. This fit right in with Dave's dream. He had done so much work around the building that I wanted to let him do whatever he wanted. People would come in on Friday nights and tell us how wonderful it was to go to a Christian nightclub. We decided to add Saturday nights and call it, "His Place".

I would be behind the coffee bar working when these band members would walk past me to set up their equipment. I could not help but gape, as they would pass by me. They had Mohawks with different color hair, tattoos, and piercings all over their bodies. I would look at them with my jaw dropped and think, "Are these people even saved?" They definitely looked like the world. When the music would start it was very loud. I couldn't hear the lyrics. I would be asking myself, "Are these even Christian songs?" They didn't sound any different than the world. These were important questions. During one of our board meetings we discussed, for three hours, how long a mosh pit should last.

I found myself very busy. I was counseling all day Monday through Friday and on nights when I wasn't teaching Boot Camp. I was also doing all of the shopping, cleaning and cooking for the coffee bar. Furthermore, Sue insisted that I needed to teach a Bible study on Monday nights after football season ended.

I was never home. I remember one day at the office, I had morning and evening appointments. I had some time in between appointments but there was not enough time for me to go home. I felt so lonely for my family I wanted to cry. I was very tired. The ministry started to suffer. That summer's Boot Camp class had dropped in attendance to four people. At one time we were up to one hundred and fifty, depending on where it was held. The *Christian nightclub* had grown in attendance to one hundred and fifty. At one point, I thought I had missed what God had called me to do. Maybe it was the *Christian nightclub* and not healing and deliverance. After all, this is what the people wanted. Most of the people that were attending did not go to church anywhere. The people's hearts were cold and hard.

The bands started setting up displays in front of the ministry to sell their "products." It had become a marketplace. Sue came to me and asked if her daughter could sell Christian T-shirts inside the ministry building. After all, the bands were selling their products outside. For some reason it did not feel right, but the way she put it, I felt I had to say, "Yes." The Christian t-shirts lasted two weeks. The third week she brought in this elaborate display to sell Jewelry.

I felt the Holy Spirit showing me what was happening. He was not happy. I remember looking at the display and feeling a ping in my heart from the Lord as though He was saying to me, "What are you doing? What are you allowing?" I quickly turned my head so I would not look at it anymore. I turned a blind eye. I felt nervous inside. I knew I should say something, but I did not want Sue to be mad at me. If she did not get what she wanted she would become very angry. So, I would walk away telling the Lord He had to deal with what was happening. I did not want her anger turned towards me.

I justified these nights as an outreach ministry to draw people in to minister to them. By the time I would get up on the platform Friday and Saturday nights to tell people about the ministry, I was so tired. After cleaning, shopping and cooking for the night, I didn't care if they got ministered to or not.

Controlling Spirit

Sue was our administrator, but at this point she had taken over the headship of the ministry. One day the volunteer staff, my husband and I came into the office and there was a "Number One" sign on her door. I thought it was a joke. It turned out she had put it there so that we all would see that she was the head of the ministry and she would hold everyone accountable to her.

Because I was so tired, I would recruit volunteers to help with different things like office work and helping behind the coffee bar. Sue always found reasons why my volunteers were not good enough to help us. There seemed to be a problem with everyone who wanted to help. When I asked where the volunteers were, Sue would tell me that she told them we didn't need them and that they should go sit down. Sue would tell me that only she and I knew how to make coffee and serve and that she and I could do it. We didn't need anyone else.

There were a few volunteers that would help no matter what. These volunteers had problems with her and she was bringing about strife and division. They would come and tell me how Sue would manipulate situations, lie and twist things in her favor. When I would call her on these matters Sue would never admit to any wrongdoing nor apologize. She would turn the situation around to be the other person's fault. I would see the lie, but the way she would twist it around, you could not prove it.

One day, Sue and I scheduled a breakfast meeting for 8:30 the following morning. I showed up right at eight-thirty. She had already arrived and was sitting in a booth. As I approached her, I could tell she was highly upset. She had a look about her that told me I had done something wrong. She was infuriated with me. Instead of, "Good morning", she started accusing me of being a half an hour late. She insisted that we said eight o'clock. I thought, "There is no way we said eight o'clock, because I did not drop my daughter off at school until 8:15." I told her I was sorry, that I must have misunderstood, and I asked her to forgive me.

I hated confrontation, so I would say: *I am sorry .....please forgive me..... I must have misunderstood. I would think things like: the buck stops here...I can say I'm sorry... I don't want to waste time auguring over who is right or wrong... Just move on.*

As I was leaving this meeting, the Lord asked, "Why did you just lie to her?" I told the Lord, "I didn't lie, God, you made me a peacemaker, and that was what I was doing, keeping the peace." The Lord said, "No, you lied. You lied, because you did not want to make her angry."

I had to start facing the fact that I would lie anytime I thought someone would be angry with me. It's not easy when the Lord starts shining His light into areas of our heart, exposing the areas that need changing - the areas we make excuses for and try to justify. The Lord brought to my mind this scripture; *you are of your father the devil, and the desires of your father you want to do. He was a murderer from the beginning, and does not stand in the truth, because there is no truth in him. When he speaks a lie, he speaks from his own resources, for he is a liar and the father of it* (John 8:44). What had I been doing, thinking I was keeping peace? Instead, I was lying because I did not want someone to be mad at me.

I didn't know it, but Sue was creating these situations to boost her favor. She would go to the volunteer staff behind my back and undermine my position. She would say things like, "You know Patti. She forgets everything. We need to pray for her. She gets everything wrong."

She made me look so incompetent. Furthermore, I was playing into it. At times I would act dumb, because I did not want conflict. People could see what was happening. They tried to tell me. I would tell them we have to walk in love and pray for her.

Sue began controlling every area of my life. I couldn't even write a newsletter without her permission and approval, because "I was not capable of writing it to her standards." When it came time to write one, I had to wait for her to make time and put me on her calendar. One time I decided I didn't need her help, so I went ahead and wrote it myself. She was very angry. You could feel it in the air. The anger was so thick it felt like you could cut it with a knife.

Benjamin and I had a date day once a week. Sue couldn't stand this. She would call me all day long for small things that could have waited. One time I let the machine pick up all the calls. By the time I answered, she was furious.

Our families would take vacations together. At first this seemed fun, but towards the end my family and I couldn't take a vacation without Sue insisting she and her family join us.

My husband is confrontational and He would call her on the things she was doing wrong. She would come to me and tell me she could not work under these circumstances and that he had to leave her alone. I would tell my husband to leave her alone, because she would get mad. Worried, I thought if she left, who would do all the paperwork? My husband was working full time and couldn't help me at the office.

Benjamin was frustrated that I let this woman control me and that I was never home. He asked me one time what would I do if I lost my family over the ministry. I thought the devil was talking to me because *I was doing the work of ministry.* Now I realize not all things we call "ministry" are really from the Lord. We can be busy doing "ministry" but never produce any fruit. *Unless the Lord builds the house, they labor in vain who build it; unless the Lord guards the city, the watchman stays awake in vain* (Psalm 127:1).

Chapter 14

Reverence/Fear of the
LORD (YAHWEH)

---❦---

The fear of the LORD is the beginning of knowledge.
(Proverbs 1:7a).

The fear of God is respecting Him, obeying Him, submitting to His discipline, and worshiping Him in awe.

One Monday morning we were fasting and praying for the ministry at the office. The presence and power of God showed up. The Lord spoke to us through me. He spoke in a bellowing voice for forty-five minutes. The power of the Holy Spirit was moving through my body in such a way I could not sit up in the chair. It was more like I was reclining in the chair. My legs were straight out in front of me and my bottom was barely on the seat. The power was so strong my body was flapping and shaking. The people in the room said I looked like a sheet out on a clothesline flapping in the wind.

The Lord said, "I never called you to entertain the church; I called you to cleanse my bride. I never called you to a coffee bar or to bring in these *Christian bands.* You take every band off of the calendar. I did not call you to come next to Dave, to help Dave with his dreams, but for Dave to come next to you to help with this anointing. You walk in an anointing and you have added things to the anointing that are not from Me. If you do not get this off of the foundation of this anointing, I will write Ichabod on the door." (Ichabod means the glory of the Lord has departed.) He spoke of many more things that had to do with what I added or took away from the anointing. While He was speaking these words to me, in my mind's eye He showed me these "bands" and Sue's daughter were selling merchandise. When He had been trying to show this to me, I would turn a blind eye and not listen to Him. He said, "My house is called a house of prayer."

Not all of the board members were there on Monday morning to hear what the Lord had said. So, I called a board meeting for Tuesday night. At the meeting the ones that had been there on Monday morning tried to explain to the others what had happened. It was like trying to explain the burning bush experience that Moses had. They also told what the Lord said. It is hard to explain a spiritual experience in ways the natural realm can understand. Truthfully, even when it happens to you, I do not think you can fully understand it. We were all pretty shaken up. After we explained what had happened, to the best of our ability, we brought out the calendar and looked through it. It was May and we had bands scheduled all the way through the end of July. After much discussion, we decided that the ministry's honor was very important. After all, we were without spot or wrinkle. We all had thoughts of, "We can not cancel all of these bands. What would people think? We are to be people of our word." Dave had signed contracts with these bands. So we decided we would let the bands that were already scheduled remain on the calendar and not add any others.

In prayer the next morning, on Wednesday after the board meeting, God spoke again to me. He was angry. He said by being people of our word, I was being disobedient to Him. Then He gave me this scripture, *So Samuel said: Has the Lord as great delight in burnt offerings and sacrifices, as in obeying the voice of the Lord? Behold, to obey is better than sacrifice, and to heed than the fat of rams. For rebellion is as the sin of witchcraft, and stubbornness is as iniquity and idolatry. Because you have rejected the word of the Lord, He also has rejected you from being king* (1 Samuel 15:22-23).

Between Him speaking to us through me during Monday Morning Prayer time at the office and what He said on Wednesday morning after the board meeting, the fear of the Lord hit me. I had been irreverent to God, manipulating His anointing any way I wanted. I had to handle His anointing HIS way.

A biblical fear of God, for the believer, is reverence. Until we understand who God is and develop a reverential fear of Him, we cannot have true wisdom. True wisdom comes only from understanding who God is.

He is holy, just, and righteous. *And now, O Israel, what does the Lord your God ask of you but to fear the Lord your God, to walk in all his ways, to love him, to serve the Lord your God with all your heart and with all your soul.... You shall fear the Lord your God you shall serve him and to him you shall hold fast, and take oaths in His name. He is your praise; he is your God, who has done for you these great and awesome things which your eyes have seen* (Deuteronomy 10:12, 20-21). The fear of God is the basis for our walking in His ways, serving Him, loving Him and having such a reverence for Him that it has an impact on the way we live our lives.

My son, do not forget my law, but let your heart keep my commands; for length of days and long life and peace they will add to you. Let not mercy and truth forsake you; bind them around your neck, write them on the tablet of your heart, and so find favor and high esteem in the sight of God and man. Trust in the Lord with all your heart, and lean not on your own understanding; in all your ways acknowledge Him, and He shall direct your paths. Do not be wise in your own eyes; Fear the Lord and depart from evil. It will be health to your flesh, and strength to your bones (Proverbs 3:1-8).

In the months leading up to that Monday morning board meeting, the Lord kept bringing to my attention King David bringing back the ark. It was God's plan for the ark to be in their midst. David went to the people and got everyone in agreement. He did everything right, except one thing: He had made a cart to carry the ark. The priests were supposed to carry the ark on their shoulders with poles. When the ark started to tumble, a man reached his hand out to catch it, and died. The second time David attempted to bring it back, he had the priests carry the Ark on poles on their shoulders. There is a crucial lesson to be learned in this story, namely that of the importance of doing God's will, God's way!

And David arose and went with all the people who were with him from Baale Judah to bring up from there the ark of God, whose name is called by the Name, the Lord of Hosts, who dwells between the cherubim. So they set the ark of God on a new cart, and brought it out of the house of Abinadab, which was on the hill; and Uzzah and Ahio, the sons of Abinadab, drove the new cart. And they brought it out of the house of Abinadab, which was on the hill, accompanying *the ark of God; and Ahio went before the ark. Then David and all the house of Israel played music before the Lord on all kinds of instruments of fir wood, on harps, on stringed instruments, on tambourines, on sistrums, and on cymbals. And when they came to Nachon's threshing floor, Uzzah put out his hand to the ark of God (Elohim) and took hold of it, for the oxen stumbled. Then the anger of the LORD (Yahweh) was aroused against Uzzah, and God struck him there for his **error**; and he died there by the ark of God. And David became angry because of the Lord's outbreak against Uzzah; and he called the name of the place Perez Uzzah to this day. David was afraid of the LORD (Yahweh) that day; and he said, "How can the ark of the Lord come to me?" So David would not move the ark of the LORD (Yahweh) with him into the City of David; but David took it aside into the house of Obed-Edom the Gittite. The ark of the Lord remained in the house of Obed-Edom the Gittite three months. And the LORD (Yahweh) blessed Obed-Edom and all his household.* (emphasis added)

Now it was told King David, saying, 'The LORD (Yahweh) has blessed the house of Obed-Edom and all that belongs to him, because of the ark of God (Elohim).'" So David went and brought up the ark of God (Elohim) from the house of Obed-Edom to the City of David with gladness. And so it was, when those bearing the ark of the LORD (Yahweh) had gone six paces, that he sacrificed oxen and fatted sheep. Then David danced before the LORD (Yahweh) with all his might; and David was wearing a linen ephod. So David and all the house of Israel brought up the ark of the LORD (Yahweh) with shouting and with the sound of the trumpet (2 Samuel 6:2-15).

Twentieth century, evangilical author, Arthur Pink wrote, "There seem to be a great many in Christendom today who are desirous of doing good, but they are exceedingly lax and careless in the mode and manner in which their desires are carried out. They act as though the means used and the methods employed mattered little or nothing, so long as their aim and end is right. They are creatures of impulse, following the dictates of mere whim and sentiment, or imitating the example of others. They seem to have no concern for *God's standard*, study not His word diligently to discover what laws and rules the Lord has given for the regulation of our conduct in His "service."

Consequently, they are governed by the flesh, rather than the Spirit, so that it frequently happens that they do good things *in a wrong way*; yea, in a manner directly opposed to *God's* way as revealed in His word." The "end does not justify the means" when you are doing ministry and serving the Lord. How we go about what we do means everything. Arthur Pink again says, "...Sooner or later all effort on the part of the "church," or of the individual Christian, which is not strictly according to the word of the Lord will prove a failure: it will be but "wood, hay, stubble" (I Cor. 3:12) in the day of divine testing and reward. God has magnified His Word above all His name (Psalm 138:2), and He demands that His servants shall do all things according to the plan and manner which He has prescribed." [9]

The Lord said the ark represents His anointing and you cannot touch His anointing any way you want. The word "error" literally means, "irreverence." The holiness of the Ark commanded that no one was to touch it. As a result of the misguided attempts to carry the Ark in their own way, Uzzah was struck dead.

A spirit of repentance hit me. What is true repentance? It is being sorry for grieving God by the way you live. It is a desire to turn from your sins without any regrets and take a new path that pleases God. The Lord started showing me everything I had been doing wrong. One of the Hebrew words for sin is *chattah* and it means "missing the mark." I had missed the mark and did not even know how far.

We had a board meeting and I was sobbing so hard I could hardly talk. I stood in front of the board and repented for everything I allowed to happen: the bands, the coffee bar, allowing *product* to be sold and *moneychangers, in His house*, when His house was to be called a house of prayer. These were good ideas not God ideas.

The Lord gave me a vision of my husband. In this vision my husband was a mile or two behind me, with his arms crossed in front of him. He was waiting to see how long it would take before I realized he no longer was walking with me. I had to repent to my husband for leaving him behind. Then the Lord said, "You left me behind also, and just like your husband, I was waiting to see how long it took before you realized that I was no longer walking with you."

The spirit of repentance hit my husband, and he started sobbing and repenting for allowing things to go as far as they had. He saw things that were wrong, but, because I didn't want to make waves with Sue, he gave up.

Through a revelation, God told me what was wrong with the Christian bands. People come into the body of Christ from the world and change the words of their worldly music to Christian lyrics. This doesn't make the music Holy. The person singing the songs had not been cleansed on the inside. It's not what goes into a man but what comes out of the heart that makes a man unclean. We, the church, need to know how to distinguish between the holy and the unholy and between the clean and the unclean.

We read about The Profane Fire of Nadab and Abihu;

Then Nadab and Abihu, the sons of Aaron, each took his censer and put fire in it, put incense on it, and offered profane fire before the Lord, which He had not commanded them. So fire went out from the Lord and devoured them, and they died before the Lord. And Moses said to Aaron, "This is what the Lord spoke, saying: 'By those who come near Me I must be regarded as holy; and before all the people I must be glorified... (Leviticus 10:1-3).

We also read, *her priests have violated My law and profaned My holy things; they have not distinguished between the holy and unholy, nor have they made known the difference between the unclean and the clean; and they have hidden their eyes from My Sabbaths, so that I am profaned among them* (Ezekiel 22:26).

Vision of a Big Ocean Liner

God gave me a vision of a big ocean liner out in the ocean. The ocean liner represents the anointing and I had taken it off course. I had gone way to the left. I had to make a quick right turn. (He said if you are one degree off, in a short distance you could be a hundred miles off.) As I made this quick right turn, I saw people hanging on to the side of the liner. Some people were falling off.

God showed me there were people that could not stay in the ministry. These changes were very hard for them. They didn't understand what God was doing. They were there for the Christian bands and the coffee bar. They wanted to be entertained.

Discerning the Wheat and Tare

I started having my eyes opened. I was questioning many things that I was seeing. We had prayer every Monday morning for an hour. In this prayer time, Sue would start praying, and she would pray fifty-five minutes of the sixty. None of us would be able to pray. We started noticing this. Instead of feeling the Holy Spirit, we would leave upset. Nothing that needed to be prayed for was being addressed. The Lord showed me she was running the clock out. Just like in a football game, one team runs the clock out, so the opponent is not able to score.

Sue would speak words that I spoke, saying all the right words you would want someone in your ministry to say. Nonetheless, something was missing. I was hearing the words I wanted to hear, but there was no anointing behind them. I remember when the Lord had caused me to become aware of this. I said to Him, "I hear her repeating the teachings almost exactly of what I am teaching. I wish everyone would learn them as well as she. Why do the words seem dead spiritually?" He said, "In a big corporation you teach verbiage to your employees. The person on the first floor, answering the phone, making minimum wage, will learn what the company wants them to say, but they don't have the heart or vision of the company. The founder of the corporation built it from the ground up. He had the vision and the heart. He wrote the book on what the verbiage for the employees should be. The employees just memorized it. She has learned your words, but she is like a parrot, just repeating what she hears."

The Lord gave me the teaching of the wheat and tares. He said the wheat produces fruit. The tare looks just like the wheat but there is no Godly fruit. The fruit that was being produced was not the fruit of the Holy Spirit.

The Lord started telling me that there was a strong demonic presence in Sue. I just couldn't believe this. She had worked so hard in the ministry. The Lord said this spirit had attached itself to me. It was after my anointing. It was there to suck me dry, to exhaust me, to stop the anointing that was on my life. I asked the Lord why Satan would be so interested in me. It was such a small ministry, nothing big. The Lord said, "Satan knows how big it is going to become. He wants to stop it when it is small." I want you to understand, I do not believe this woman is Satan. I do, however, believe that Satan and demons can use us, when we have brokenness and when we try to do God's work in the flesh.

Chapter 15

Understanding Spiritual Authority

—⊷⟨◈⟩⊶—

*T*he Lord said He had given me delegated authority over this anointing. I did not know what delegated authority was. I had never heard the term before. Many in the body of Christ today do not know what it is. It is not having control over others and demanding they submit to your authority or else. He said He was holding me accountable for everything that happens in and to this anointing. It does not matter what other people do or don't do. I am responsible for the anointing that the Lord placed on my life. The Lord forced me to take my position back. I had to start taking my delegated authority. I had to start by holding this woman accountable to what she was doing in the ministry. *Obey your leaders and submit to them, for they keep watch over your lives, as people who will have to render an account. So make it a task of joy for them, not one of groaning; for that is of no advantage to you* (Hebrews 13:17 CJB).

The Lord had me study delegated authority. As I was studying it I came across Watchman Nee's book, "Spiritual Authority".

The Throne Of God (Elohim) Established Upon Authority

"God's works issue from God's throne; God's throne is established upon authority. All things have been created by the authority of God, and all laws on earth are held together through authority. Hence, the Bible says that God upholds all things by the word, which is of His authority (Heb. 1:3b). It does not say that God upholds all things

by His power. God's authority represents God Himself; God's power only represents God's works. It is easy to be forgiven of sin against God's (Elohim) power, but it is not that easy to be forgiven of sin against God's authority, because sinning against God's authority is sinning against God Himself. In the whole universe only God is authority. All other authorities are appointed by God. Nothing is greater than authority in the universe; nothing can surpass it. For this reason, if we want to serve God, we must know God's (Elohim) authority.

Satan's Beginning

Satan became Satan because he overstepped God's authority. He wanted to compete with God and to stand in opposition to God. Rebellion is the cause of the fall of Satan.

Both Isaiah 14:12-15 and Ezekiel 28:13-17 speak of the transgression and the fall of Satan. Isaiah 14 tells us that Satan violated God's authority, while Ezekiel 28 tells us that he violated God's holiness. Violating God's authority is a matter of rebellion; it is more serious than violating God's holiness. Sin is a matter of conduct; it is easy to be forgiven of sin. But rebellion is a matter of principle; it is not easy to be forgiven of rebellion. Satan, in trying to set up his throne above that of God's, violated God's authority. The principle of Satan is the principle of self-exaltation. Sin's coming into being was not the cause of Satan's fall. Rather, Satan's rebellion against God's authority, for which he was condemned by God, subsequently gave rise to sin.

Hence, if we want to serve God, we can never violate the matter of authority. To do so is to follow the principle of Satan. We can never preach the word of Christ under the principle of Satan. There is a possibility in God's work that we can stand in principle on Satan's side, while we stand in doctrine on Christ's side. All the while, we may think that we are still doing the Lord's work.

Submitting to God's Direct Authority and Also Submitting to His Deputy Authority

Many think that they have submitted themselves to God already. They do not know that they still need to submit to God's deputy authority. Those who are truly submissive see God's authority in all environments—in their homes and in all institutions...."[10]

The Spirit of Intimidation

For God has not given us a spirit of fear, but of power and of love and of a sound mind (2 Timothy 1:7).

The Lord started showing me I have delegated authority, but I walked in a spirit of intimidation. Furthermore, because of the spirit of intimidation, I had given my delegated authority over to someone else. I had fear of man, rejection, abandonment, and anger. When the Lord began revealing this to me, He began showing me flashes from my childhood, and how, as a little girl living in an abusive home, the doorway was opened for these spirits to set up strongholds. I had to break the spirit of intimidation over me. While I was under this spirit, it stopped the anointing. I had been walking in fear of man and not Fear (Reverence) of God.

False Peace and False Unity

I hated confrontation, and when Sue would call me into her office to confront me on an issue, I would start getting nervous, and my stomach would become all shaky. I would think, "*Oh no, not again. What did I do wrong* this time?" I hated the thought of someone being upset with me. When I was growing up, when someone was angry, people got beat up. The very thought that someone was mad made me want to run the other way. When Sue would confront me, I would tell her whatever she wanted to hear, so she wouldn't be angry. I would say I was sorry for things I never did wrong. I would say, "Yes" when I wanted to say, "No." When I was being confronted my mind would turn to mush. I was unable to think clearly. I was always searching my heart and praying for God to change me, so I wouldn't upset her. I never questioned if she was wrong.

I would rationalize and tell myself I was keeping peace. After all, didn't the Lord say blessed are the peacekeepers? God showed me that there are spirits of false peace and false unity. Even though on the surface I was keeping peace and unity, I had no peace in my soul. Neither did the other people who were having problems with Sue. I would leave the ministry upset. At night I would try to go to sleep. Instead, I would toss and turn knowing something was wrong, but not knowing how to fix it. There was no unity even though I pretended that there was. As soon as Sue walked in the room she brought division and strife. I pretended there was peace and unity, because I didn't know what else to do.

I would avoid anything that involved **confrontation**, thinking that it was "unchristian." After all I was a **peacekeeper**. *Yeshua* said, "Blessed are the peacemakers..." not the peacekeepers.

In *Breaking Intimidation* by John Bevere, here is what is taught:

"**A peacekeeper** avoids confrontation at any cost. He will go to any length to preserve a false sense of security, which he mistakes for peace.

*A **peacemaker** will boldly confront no matter what the cost is to him. He is motivated by his love for God and truth. Real peace only thrives in these conditions. The Kingdom of God is a Kingdom of peace – but does not come from the absence of confrontation. Yeshua said, "The kingdom of heaven suffers violence, and the violent take it by force." (Matthew 11:12b). There is violent opposition to the Kingdom of God (Elohim) advancing–always!*
We can't ignore situations and think they will go away. What we do not confront will not change!"

The Lord told me this was a demon and I could not have peace or unity with a demon. He showed me that the demons were laughing at me. As Sue would walk away the demons were saying, "We can make Patty do whatever we want." It was like a chess game for the demons.

The spirit of intimidation is here to silence us. As the Lord revealed the spirit of intimidation he also revealed that, along with intimidation, there are spirits to silence us. He showed me that growing up in a dysfunctional home, I did not have a voice to say, no...I don't like that...there is something wrong...etc. There was an assignment from Satan to cause me to have no voice. If we don't have a voice we can't speak what God wants us to speak. If we are walking in intimidation we will fear man and not speak the truth in love.

Intimidation is in fact a spirit, a spirit that is sent by Satan. *God has not given us a spirit of fear, but of power and of love and of a sound mind* (2 Timothy 1:7). Since the enemy sends this spirit, we know that the ultimate agenda of this spirit is "to kill, steal and destroy" all of mankind, especially the saints of God.

The key to overcoming fear is total and complete trust in God. Sometimes we are afraid; sometimes this "spirit of fear" overcomes us. To overcome it we need to trust in and love God completely. *Trust in the Lord with all your heart, and lean not on your own understanding; in all your ways acknowledge Him, and He shall direct your paths* (Proverbs 3:5-6).

We are encouraged, for example, *Fear not, for I am with you; be not dismayed, for I am your God. I will strengthen you, yes, I will help you I will uphold you with My righteous right hand* (Isaiah 41:10).

The Lord said I was bringing confusion to my volunteer staff. They were losing respect and trust in my leadership ability. They would come and tell me things Sue was doing wrong, but I would not deal with the issues because of her anger. I thought I was walking in love, peace and unity. When you don't know how to be a leader and you want peace at all cost, you bring confusion and mistrust to the people God (*Elohim*) has put under you as a leader. This can be in any area not just ministry. It can be in your home or business.

As the Lord started breaking intimidation off of me, He had me take the headship back. I had to stand in my Delegated Authority that God had given me. Not only did I have fear of man, but I had fear that I couldn't do what God wanted me to do. I had never walked this way before. I felt, and still do, like the least of the least of them. So when the Lord was trying to have me grow in my anointing, instead of going to Him, I ran to man.

Thus says the Lord: 'Cursed is the man who trusts in man and makes flesh his strength, whose heart departs from the Lord. For he shall be like a shrub in the desert, and shall not see when good comes, but shall inhabit the parched places in the wilderness, in a salt land which is not inhabited. Blessed is the man who trusts in the Lord, and whose hope is the Lord. For he shall be like a tree planted by the waters, which spreads out its roots by the river, and will not fear when heat comes; But its leaf will be green, and will not be anxious in the year of drought, nor will cease from yielding fruit (Jeremiah 17:5-8).

God wanted me to be the tree planted by waters, but I had become a tumbleweed in the desert. I had to start trusting God and not man. The day at my house, when we had the meeting with the adviser on how to start a non-profit, fear hit me. I didn't think I would be able to keep good records for the IRS. Sue said, "I can do that." It was at that point I took my eyes off of God and put them on her.

Taking the headship back meant I had to start becoming the leader and not be led by her. I had to quit allowing her to dictate to me and hold me accountable. This was very hard at first. The Lord taught me that I didn't have to always have confrontation. I could communicate, and I had to start speaking the truth in love.

Chapter 16

The Importance of Boundaries

ecause I grew up in a dysfunctional home, I had no boundaries. I didn't even know what boundaries were. I had never heard this word either. When I was growing up I could never tell people no. Because I was the youngest of five children and I was my father's only biological child, I was his favorite. He would give me things that he would not give to the other children. So, when they would want something, they would ask me to go get it. Most of the time, I would get it willingly. But, there were other times when I would not want to go and ask. These were the times that my siblings would put pressure on me until I did what they wanted. My mother used her emotions to control me. If I did not do the things she asked, she would become depressed even suicidal. So I would give in, thinking it was my fault if she was not happy all the time. It made me feel very selfish when I did not want to do what she or others wanted me to do. I did not have boundaries, and I did not say no. That is why I was molested so many times.

Around the time the Lord was showing me all of this, someone gave me the book, *Boundaries,* by Dr. Henry Cloud and Dr. John Townsend. It seems that I go through life lessons first, then the LORD has someone give me a book or I hear a message or teaching on what I happen to be going through or just went through. I highly recommend this book.

Boundaries, by Dr. Henry Cloud and Dr. John Townsend instructs us:

"Learning to set healthy personal boundaries is necessary for maintaining a positive self-concept, or self-image. It is our way of communicating to others that we have self-respect, self-worth, and will not allow others to define us.

Personal boundaries are the physical, emotional, mental and spiritual limits we establish to protect ourselves from being manipulated, used, or violated by others. They allow us to separate who we are, and what we think and feel, from the thoughts and feelings of others. Their presence helps us express ourselves as the unique individuals we are, while we acknowledge the same in others.

It is not possible to enjoy healthy relationships without the existence of personal boundaries, or without our willingness to communicate them directly and honestly with others. We must recognize that each of us is a unique individual with distinct emotions, needs and preferences. This is equally true for our spouses, children and friends.

A boundary is a personal property line that marks those things for which we are responsible. Boundaries define who we are and who we are not. They preserve our integrity, causing us to take responsibility for who we are, and to take control of our life." [11]

After I read this book I could see that I had to start setting boundaries. It was hard at first, because I had been under a spirit of intimidation, and I did not have a voice. As the Lord delivered me of intimidation, He had me pray for my voice. There were demons assigned to stop me from having a voice. When I would be hurt emotionally, or someone was mad at me, it felt like I had the wind knocked out of me. I could not speak. When I was confronted, I would feel confused, and I could not think of what I should say. When the confrontation was over, my mind could think clearly, and I would think of the things I should have said but did not.

The Lord had set me free from the spirit of intimidation and gave me my voice. He taught me boundaries. Now I had to set boundaries and confront issues.

One of the first things the Lord had me do is add International to the name Without Spot or Wrinkle Ministries. At this time I had run out of business cards and needed to reorder them. The Lord said, "I want you to add "International" to the name on your cards. I have called you to the nations, and I told you at the beginning to put International on the name." When I asked Sue to order them and told her what the Lord said, she started giving me all kinds of excuses; it would be too hard to go back and change the name legally, it would cost too much. It would take too much time. Then she asked, "You really do not want to do all of that do you?"

I decided I had to bypass her. I had a friend do all of the legal work, which turned out to be very little. Once Sue found out I had someone else do the work, she was upset and said she did not know how I got the idea she did not want to make the changes. She said she would have been happy to change the name. Sue now had to be accountable for the things she was doing wrong in the ministry. She never repented or submitted to my authority. Things got worse before they got better.

Sue had been counseling a pregnant woman living with her boyfriend. The woman wanted to be married before she gave birth to her child. Since the couple had no money for a wedding Sue asked if I would perform the ceremony pro bono. I agreed to officiate the ceremony in my office with two or three witnesses. This usually takes fifteen to twenty minutes. Normally my honorarium is two hundred and fifty dollars. This includes a personalized wedding ceremony, counseling before and after the ceremony and the hours that I need to be at the ceremony before and after the nuptials.

Things began to go awry very quickly. Sue informed me on the Thursday night prior to the Saturday wedding, that the plans had changed. Instead of having it in my office with two or three witnesses, they were now planning on a full-blown wedding with forty people in attendance. They would be decorating the ministry building the night before and they also planned a reception at the ministry building following the ceremony. This was not what we had agreed on. It now would require at least ten hours of my time instead of fifteen to twenty minutes in my office. Sue reassured me I did not need to come in the Friday night prior to the wedding. Sue's daughter had been hired to decorate and Sue would come in to help her. She made a comment in passing, "People were coming in and dropping off handfuls of money."

As I drove home I had a feeling in the pit of my stomach, I felt something was wrong, I just didn't know what. I went to bed upset. How was I going to handle this situation?

I officiated the wedding on Saturday and spent the day at the reception. I also cleaned up afterwards. I was upset but still did not know why. The words Sue had said kept going through my mind. "People were coming in and dropping off handfuls of money." How did they go from no money, to hiring her daughter to decorate?

She told me on Monday that the young couple that got married gave her a check for two hundred dollars, and she was going to give me fifty for officiating the wedding. She was going to give the ministry fifty and she was going to give herself a hundred. I asked her why she was paying herself a hundred dollars. She said, "I bought decorations and I am reimbursing myself for them." As I left her office, things bothered me even more. I couldn't put my finger on it. As I kept praying about it, I sensed the Lord telling me to ask for receipts. I needed an account of everything that came in and everything that went out. So I called her phone, but she didn't answer. I left a message on her voicemail informing her I needed receipts and an account of every penny coming in and going out. I wanted them on my desk by the following Monday. When Monday arrived, she came in with some receipts in her hand. She was furious. We went into my office and as she sat in front of me, she kept waving the receipts around in the air yelling at me. She said, "This wedding and the money that came in has nothing to do with the ministry."

I told her every penny that came in and went out had everything to do with the ministry. At this point, I asked her to leave the ministry. Things had changed so much between us both. It was no longer comfortable. I was now stepping up to my position.

Jezebel

God started showing me that I had been fighting a principality not a person. We hear in churches all the time that a person has a "Jezebel spirit." Jezebel was a person that demons were able to operate through. But, our battle is not with flesh and blood. *For we do not wrestle against flesh and blood, but against principalities, against powers, against the rulers of the darkness of this age, against spiritual hosts of wickedness in the heavenly places* (Ephesians 6:12).

Principalities are understood by the Greek word *arche* meaning chief or ruler, these principalities are ruling devil spirits possessing executive authority or governmental rule in the world. As we will see, this ruling power usually involves a particular nation, people or race. There are evil angels ruling the kingdoms of the world that oppose the truth of God. Satan is the chief prince or ruler, of both the world system and its organization of demons.

Someone gave me a book by Juanita Bynum, called *My Spiritual Inheritance*. God revealed to me, through this book and my own research, the principality behind Jezebel is Ashtoreth. This principality moves into action when a person is intimidated into giving up their delegated authority.

When Sue was confronted about taking my authority, she told me she never took it but, that I gave it to her. She was right! I had no knowledge of my delegated authority, and I gave it away.

So who is Ashtoreth? I remember reading about Ashtoreth in the Old Testament along with Baal worship, so I went back to the Old Testament to study this.

All through the Old Testament, the children of Israel kept getting in trouble with God because of this worship. King Solomon, the wisest King on earth, lost the kingdom because of pagan wives who caused him to worship Ashtoreth. God had warned the children of Israel not to marry pagan wives, because they would cause His children to stray away from Him and worship pagan gods. King Ahab of Israel did evil in the sight of the Lord, more evil than all the other Kings of Israel, because he took Jezebel in marriage and went and served Baal. Not only did he serve Baal, but now Satan was sitting on the throne of Israel through this woman.

Satan proclaimed that he would be like the Most High God, and he would sit on the mount of the congregation We read, *In the thirty-eighth year of Asa king of Judah Ahab the son of Omri became king over Israel; and Ahab the son of Omri reigned over Israel in Samaria twenty-two years Now Ahab the son of Omri did evil in the sight of the Lord, more than all who were before him And it came to pass, as though it had been a trivial thing for him to walk in the sins of the son of Nebat that he took as wife the daughter of Ethbaal, king of the Sidonians; and he went and served Baal and worshipped him. Then he set up an altar for Baal in the temple of Baal, which he had built in Samaria. And Ahab*

Smith's Bible Dictionary defines **Ashtoreth**: "A goddess of the Phoenicians and Canaanites. The name occurs in South Arabic as Athtar, a god identified with the planet Venus. In the Ras Shamra tablets are found the masculine 'Athtar and the feminine' Athtart. In the Amarna letters this goddess is known as Ashtartu. In Babylonia Ishtar whose name is cognate with Ashtarte (Ashtart), was identified with Venus. She was the goddess of sexual love (perversion), maternity, and fertility.

115

did more to provoke the Lord God of Israel to anger than all the kings of Israel who were before him (1 Kings 16:29-33).

Jezebel was a Pagan Princess. Her father was the king of the Zidonians. But who were these people? They were the inhabitants of Zidon. They were among the nations of Canaan who were left to give the Israelites practice in the art of war. They oppressed the Israelites on their first entrance into the country (Judges 10:12). They were idolaters, and worshiped Ashtoreth as their goddess, (I Kings 11:5, 33; II Kings 23:13) as well as the sun god Baal from whom their king was named. (I Kings 16:31) Jezebel fed the prophets of Baal and Ashtoreth at her own table.

"Prostitution as a religious rite in the service of this goddess, who appears under various names, is widely attested. The identification of 'Ashtart with Aphrodite is evidence of her sexual character."

In Revelation 2, we see someone else named Jezebel mentioned as the false prophet. ... *you allow that woman Jezebel, who calls herself a prophetess, to teach and to seduce my servants to commit sexual immorality and to eat things sacrificed to idols. And I gave her time to repent of her sexual immorality and she did not repent. Indeed, I will cast her into a sick bed, and those who commit adultery with her into great tribulation, unless they repent of their deeds* (Revelation 2:20b-22).

I believe now, John was speaking of the demons that operated through this "woman" when he called her Jezebel.

Usurping Authority

Satan seeks to neutralize true spiritual authority. No enemy from hell does this more efficiently than the principality of Ashtoreth. This principality targets Spiritual leaders that have been called to do great exploits for the Kingdom of God, leaders who are responsible for steering the ship toward God's intended vision. When Ashtoreth attacks a leader and a church, any or all of the following may be involved:

- Witchcraft
- Intimidation/fear
- Discouragement
- Usurping delegated spiritual authority
- Physical sickness

116

The **Ashtoreth** principality seeks control through manipulation. It has a deep hatred of true spiritual authority, and uses anything to gain control of this authority in pursuit of power: emotional pressure, witchcraft and obsessive sensuality to name a few. It uses subtle persuasion to gain influence and get close to those in true authority. It then uses this position to gradually intimidate and dominate. It likes to use the power and influence of others to accomplish its goals and control its environment. *Jezebel wrote letters in Ahab's name and sealed them with his seal, and sent them to the elders and nobles who were dwelling in the city... .* (1 Kings 21:8). This is typical of this spirit. It prefers to remain concealed in the background, while it manipulates situations and leaders.

In Hebrew, the name Jezebel means "without cohabitation." She will not live or "cohabit" with those she cannot dominate and control. She will have no equal. Control is what **Ashtoreth** wants more than anything. Even when **Ashtoreth** appears to be submissive, it is usually out of a carefully wrought plan to gain influence.

Ashtoreth is stubborn, prideful arrogant, and unwilling to repent of its ungodly behavior and influence upon the people of God. It must be dealt with firmly.

Ashtoreth's greatest enemy is true spiritual authority. As Jezebel opposed Elijah, so Ashtoreth today opposes spiritual authority. It continues to threaten, by manipulation and intimidation, to spiritually kill the true prophets. Elijah was a man under God's (*Elohim*) protection for many years. The power of God (*Elohim*) worked through him. In spite of all that he accomplished as a powerful man of God (*Elohim*), Jezebel intimidated Elijah. This is a powerful demonic force not to be taken lightly.

Ashtoreth is a murderous spirit. It wants to alter world history. It stops at nothing to destroy God's (*Elohim*) inheritance.

Yeshua is the head of the Church. Believers are the body. If all things (including Satan and his religious structure) are under the feet of *Yeshua*, then they are also under our feet because we are the body. Under the feet means they are under *Yeshua's* power and authority, which God (*Elohim*) has delegated to us. *Yeshua* said He has given us authority over *all the power of the enemy.* (Luke 10:19) This includes spiritual wickedness in high places.

And he who overcomes, and keeps My works until the end, to him I will give power over the nations (Revelation 2:26). We have power over Jezebel.

The Royal Offspring of David

Jezebel and Ahab had a daughter Athaliah. She married Jehoram, King of Judah. (2 Kings 8:18, 26) She had a hatred for legitimate and godly authority, going to extremes to destroy all opposition. She tried to murder all her male descendants to ensure her **illegitimate authority** to the throne of Judah, almost destroying the entire destiny of those called to rule and reign on the throne of God (*Elohim*).

Athaliah succeeded in killing all the royal offspring except for Joash. Jehoshabeath, the daughter of King Ahaziah, hid Joash away from the other sons who were being killed. Joash was later crowned King of Judah by the congregation of Levites and chief fathers of Israel under the leadership of Jehoiada, a priest. Had Joash himself been murdered with the rest of the royal offspring from David, the divine lineage would have been destroyed. We realize the magnitude of this historical event when we remember that *Yeshua*, the Messiah, was to be a descendent of David.

Satan and his principalities are after those who keep the commandments of God (*Elohim*) and have the testimony of *Yeshua. And the dragon was enraged with the woman, and he went to make war with the rest of her offspring, who keep the commandments of God (Elohim) and have the testimony of Jesus (Yeshua) Christ* (Revelation 12:17). This scripture is referring to Israel and the believers that have been grafted into Israel.

This spirit goes after the generational inheritance. The spirit that operated through Athaliah targets and attacks the generations in order to ultimately destroy a people and a nation.

We can see, as an example, this spirit working through the Roman Emperor Nero. He murdered and persecuted thousands of Christians, and was accused of murdering his own mother and wife, and some of his advisors.

Adolf Hitler seduced an entire nation to elect him as leader over Germany. Once he attained that power, he legalized genocide in the countries he defeated and ruled. He murdered millions of Jews as well as many other "undesirables." He attempted to destroy all living Jews – the destruction of an entire generation and race - while aggressively seeking world domination.

Today we are seeing this spirit in Islam. Allah is the moon god. The moon god is none other then Ashtoreth, who persecutes and kills Jews and Christians, along with all "infidels" who will not submit to and come under its control. It uses intimidation to control.

Before Athaliah's seventh year as queen, the priest Jehoiada seized the opportunity to place Joash, descendant of David and heir to the throne, into his rightful position. He secretly aligned military forces to protect Joash. In a secret Temple ceremony, Joash was crowned king. (II Chronicles 23)

God always preserves a righteous seed – a remnant – to fulfill His perfect will. We need to pray for those seeds of righteousness to be divinely protected from the enemy's plans!

It took a king to take down Jezebel. It was a priest who took down her daughter. *Yeshua* made us kings and priest as we read, *John, to the seven churches which are in Asia: Grace to you and peace from Him who is and who was and who is to come, and from the seven Spirits who are before His throne, and from Jesus Christ, the faithful witness, the firstborn from the dead, and the ruler over the kings of the earth. To Him who loved us and washed us from our sins in His own blood, and has made us kings and priests to His God (Elohim) and Father, to Him be glory and dominion forever and ever. Amen* (Revelation 1:4-6).

Everything I experienced with Sue was meant to teach me that these principalities are very much alive today. They go from generation to generation and do not die. Satan can transform himself into an angel of light. *For such are false apostles, deceitful workers, transforming themselves into apostles of Christ. And no wonder! For Satan himself transforms himself into an angel of light. Therefore it is no great thing if his ministers also transform themselves into ministers of righteousness, whose end will be according to their works* (II Corinthians 11:13-15).

Paganism

I asked the Lord how this entered into the ministry. How could this come in and operate without me knowing it? This is a deliverance ministry.... How could it stay? What gave it legal rights to be here?

The Lord said it is in the foundation of our existing religious system. Then he reminded me that when I minister to someone I get a history of that person. Knowing the foundation is necessary to restore his or her soul realm. I had to look at the history of the church. I remembered, in the Old Testament, I read about Baal and Ashtoreth. But what had they to do with us today?

119

How does Paganism influence the Body of Christ today?

The Easter Celebration

As I was studying about Ashtoreth and Baal on Easter morning 2005, I was shocked at what I found, as I read in the International Standard Bible Encyclopedia, about Easter .The English word comes from the Anglo-Saxon Eastre or Estera. Eostre, is also known as Ashtoreth, or Astarte or Ishtar, a Teutonic goddess to whom sacrifice was offered in April. So the name was transferred from the *pashcal* (Passover) feast, which was also the anniversary of Christ's death and resurrection. When I read this, I felt like I had been punched in the stomach. The Christian celebration of Christ's death and resurrection is linked to the Jewish celebration of the Passover. How did the word Easter come to be associated with the festival of Passover? The Babylonian idol Ishtar (pronounced in the original language as *Easter*, but also known as Astarte and Ashtoreth), was worshipped by pagan Romans, Greeks and some Israelites. Ashtoreth is also known as the "Queen of Heaven."

This is a principality and enemy of God. Satan has always sought to get the world to worship him instead of God. The Queen of Heaven had appeared under several names in several places long before Christ was born in the flesh.

Worship of the "Queen of Heaven" involved idols and sun worship.

*"Therefore do not pray for this people, nor lift up a cry or prayer for them, nor make intercession to Me; for I will not hear you. Do you not see what they do in the cities of Judah and in the streets of Jerusalem? The children gather wood, the fathers kindle the fire, and the women knead dough, to make cakes for the **queen of heaven;** and they pour out drink offerings to other gods, that they may provoke Me to anger.* (Jeremiah 7:16-18) (emphasis added)

So I went in and saw, and there—every sort of creeping thing, abominable beasts, and all the idols of the house of Israel, portrayed all around on the walls. And there stood before them seventy men of the elders of the house of Israel, and in their midst stood Jaazaniah the son of Shaphan. Each man had a censer in his hand, and a thick cloud of incense went up. Then He said to me, "Son of man, have you seen what the elders of the house of Israel do in the dark, every man in the room of his idols? For they say, 'The Lord does not see us, the Lord has forsaken the land.'" And He said to me, "Turn again, and you will see greater abominations that they are doing." So He brought me to the door of the north gate of the Lord's house; and to my dismay, women were sitting there weeping for Tammuz. Then He said to me, "Have you seen this, O son of man? Turn again, you will see greater abominations than these." So He brought me into the inner court of the Lord's house; and there, at the door of the temple of the Lord, between the porch and the altar, were about twenty-five men with their backs toward the temple of the Lord and their faces toward the east, and they were worshiping the sun toward the east" (Ezekiel 8:10-16).

They forsook the LORD (Yahweh) and served Baal and the Ashtoreth's. And the anger of the LORD (Yahweh) was hot against Israel. So He delivered them into the hands of plunderers who despoiled them; and He sold them into the hands of their enemies all around, so that they could no longer stand before their enemies (Judges 2:13-14).

When did this worship begin?

Nimrod, Semiramis and Tammuz

Nimrod was the founder of a great false religious system that can be traced back to Genesis. It began in ancient Babylon and has always opposed the truth of God. Much of the Babylonian worship was carried on through mysterious symbols—thus the "Mystery" religion.

This system of idolatry spread from Babylon to the nations. It was from this location that men were scattered over the face of the earth (Gen. 11:9). As they went from Babylon, they took their occult worship and its various mystery symbols with them."

In Hebrew and Christian tradition, Nimrod is considered the leader of those who built the Tower of Babel in the land of Shinar, though the Bible never actually states this. Nimrod's kingdom included the cities of Babel, Erech, Accad, and Calneh, all in Shinar (Genesis 10:10).

Ancient writings showed he was so evil that, it is said he married his own mother, whose name was Semiramis. After Nimrod's untimely death, Semiramis propagated the evil doctrine of Nimrod's survival as a spirit being. After Nimrod died, Semiramis became pregnant. She attributed her pregnancy to the rays of the sun, as though Nimrod had become the sun god and thus had impregnated her. She bore a son whom she named Tammuz, "Mother and Child" (Semiramis and Tammuz), according to the Babylonian tradition. She claimed that Tammuz was Nimrod reborn, the son of the sun god. **This was a satanic deception foretold in the Garden of Eden, of the promise of a coming Savior. (Genesis 3:15).** The birth of Tammuz was, of course, another part of the satanic lie. Semiramis claimed that her son was supernaturally conceived, so the mother was worshiped as well as the child. Many of the Jews in Babylon accepted, at least in part, this satanic religion, naming one of their Jewish months Tammuz. This worship of "Mother and Child" spread over the world. The names varied in different countries and languages. In Egypt it was Isis and Osiris; in Asia, Cybele and Deolus; in Rome, Fortuna and Jupiter. Names are found even in Greece, China, Japan, and Tibet. The counterpart of the Madonna is found long before the birth of Christ!

Through her scheming and designing, Semiramis became the Babylonian "Queen of Heaven." Nimrod, under various names, became the "divine son of heaven." Through the generations, in this idolatrous worship, Nimrod also became the false Messiah, Baal the sun god.

His son was Tammuz, spoken of in the Bible (Ezekiel 8:14). Tammuz, son of the mighty hunter, died at the age of forty while hunting. He was gored by a wild boar. This was the basis for a tradition to fast for forty days in his honor. Each day commemorated one year of his life. Unbeknown to many Christians, ham is eaten on Easter to commemorate his death by goring.

From Babylon this mystery religion spread to all the surrounding nations with its pagan symbols. Everywhere the cult of the mother and the child became the popular system. Their worship was celebrated with the most disgusting and immoral practices. The image of the Queen of Heaven with the babe in her arms was seen everywhere, though the names differ as languages differed. It became the mystery religion of Phoenicia: They carried the mystery religion to the ends of the earth.

The Christmas Celebration

"When *Yeshua* was born, the mystery of iniquity was holding sway everywhere, except where the truth of God (*Elohim*), as revealed in the Old Testament, was known. Thus, when the early Christians set out upon the great task of carrying the gospel to the end of the earth, they found themselves everywhere confronted by this system in one form or another. Though Babylon as a city had long been but a memory, her mysteries had not died with her.

The winter solstice occurs on December 21, and Saturnalia was kept from December 17-24. Then on December 25, Brumalia was the celebration of the rebirth of the sun god called Mithraism Worship of Sol, the sun god, was a continuation of Baal worship from ancient days. It was present in Egypt and ancient Babylon. December 25 is the birthday of Tammuz, the son of Semiramis, and the rebirth of Nimrod.

The ancient legend is that a green tree sprang up on Brumalia, with the stump symbolizing Nimrod (Baal) and the green tree Tammuz.

The northern Europeans worshiped the same gods from ancient Babylon, but under the name Odin. Odin was the equivalent of Sol (Baal). The ever- green fir tree was sacred to Odin and people decorated it during the festival of Saturnalia. *For the customs of the peoples are futile; For one cuts a tree from the forest, the work of the hands of the workman, with the ax. They decorate it with silver and gold; They fasten it with nails and hammers so that it will not topple* (Jeremiah 10:3-4). Legend has it that Odin would bestow yuletide gifts to those who approached the sacred fir tree on Brumalia.

The giving of presents on December 25 happened long before Rome, under Constantine. He arbitrarily chose December 25 as the supposed birthday of *Yeshua*." 12

After the Lord showed me Christmas was Baal's birthday and Easter was celebrated for Ashtoreth, thus both were pagan, I was devastated. When I read the Old Testament, I think, *how could ancient Israel worship Baal and Ashtoreth when God kept telling them it was an abomination?* Jeremiah warned the people of the Lord's judgment coming as a consequence of their sin of worshipping Baal and Ashtoreth. We see they did not understand.

And it shall be, when you show this people all these words, and they say to you, 'Why has the Lord pronounced all this great disaster against us? Or what is our iniquity? Or what is our sin that we have committed ...Against the Lord our God?' then you shall say to them, 'Because your fathers have forsaken Me,' says the Lord; 'they have walked after other gods and have served them and worshiped them, and have forsaken Me and not kept My law. And you have done worse than your fathers, for behold, each one follows the dictates of his own evil heart, so that no one listens to Me (Jeremiah 16:10-12).

I have heard, over the years, many pastors say, "We know Christmas is pagan, but it does not matter to God if we change it and make it the birth of Jesus."

Satan said he would be like the Most High God. He would sit on the mount of the congregation. (The name for church is ecclesia the called-out ones, or congregation.) Through these pagan days he has been doing just that.

How you are fallen from heaven, O Lucifer, son of the morning! How you are cut down to the ground, you who weakened the nations! For you have said in your heart: 'I will ascend into heaven, I will exalt my throne above the stars of God; I will also sit on the mount of the congregation the farthest sides of the north; I will ascend above the heights of the clouds, I will be like the Most High' (Isaiah 14:12-14).

Years earlier, I had started praying for God to give me answers to questions I did not know how to ask. It started one day when I was out running errands.

I received some knowledge that I didn't know existed. I was so excited to find out this information. It was an "Aha!" moment. A light went on. When I got home, I went bouncing into the house to share with Benjamin what I learned that day. With great excitement, I shared it. To my surprise his response was, "Why didn't you ask me? I knew that." I went away talking to God, "That's not fair God. If I don't know information exists, then how can I ask? Your word says I have not because I ask not. Okay God, then I ask ahead of time, give me the answers to questions I do not know how to ask. Then let me be able to receive those answers."

Finding out all this information, I wanted to click the delete button on my computer, and pretend that I never read any of this. Then I heard the voice of the Lord say to me, "You have asked for truth. You prayed for Me to give you answers to questions you never knew how to ask, and to let you be able to receive those answers." I had prayed that prayer, but I did not expect to find out what I had been doing was pagan. Not only pagan, but this was a demonic principality that had come in next to me in the ministry to destroy the anointing that is on my life.

That Easter morning in 2005, I felt a lot of emotions. The realization that these principalities and demons go from one generation to the next caused me to feel sick. I felt like I had been punched in the stomach. They do not die. As spirits, they re-invent themselves so we will worship them instead of God without being aware of what we are doing. I felt fear. What would people say when I shared with them what I found out? I shut down my computer and went into the living room where Benjamin and Michelle were sitting. I felt compelled to share this information with them. I had already shared with Benjamin what the Lord had me studying about Jezebel. It was a strong spiritual battle we had been in. As soon as I shared this information, Benjamin said, "We have to quit celebrating these then." Michelle was very upset that I told them Christmas was pagan and so was Easter. Her first response was, "What about the presents?" I told her the Lord showed me it was not Jesus' birthday, and she informed me she already knew that. For her it had nothing to do with Jesus. It was all about the presents.

Fear hit me. The spirit of intimidation tried to come back. My First thoughts were, "Oh no, my in-laws are going to be really mad at me." In Benjamin's family you do not mess with tradition no matter what.

That day we had already committed ourselves to go to my daughter Pamela's house for Easter. We discussed if we should keep this commitment, since I had now discovered this information. We decided to keep our commitment. When Pamela had invited us she made it clear she did not want me preaching. She said I could pray for the meal but it had to be a short prayer.

When we arrived, people were already drinking. I sat and watched, observing the people that had come to this party, contemplating everything I just learned. I watched as two people on her front porch toasted one another with their mixed alcoholic drinks, and declared, "Happy Easter." My heart sunk. How was this glorifying our Heavenly Father?

I kept this in my heart for awhile, not sharing it with anyone other than Benjamin and Michelle.

Along with Boot Camp Basic Training, I had been teaching a class called Strategies Of The Enemy. As with any teaching, I wait on the Lord to hear what He wants taught. He wanted me to teach the information He gave me about Christmas and Easter. Again, intimidation tried to come back. The Lord reminded me of reverence for Him. He gave me the scripture, *"Woman, believe Me, the hour is coming when you will neither on this mountain, nor in Jerusalem, worship the Father.*

You worship what you do not know; we know what we worship, for salvation is of the Jews. But the hour is coming, and now is, when the true worshippers will worship the Father In spirit and truth, for the Father Is seeking such to worship Him. God is Spirit, and those who worship Him must worship in spirit and truth." (John 4:21-24).

Yeshua was speaking to a Samaritan woman, when he said you do not know what you worship. But the day is coming you will worship in spirit and in truth.

Who are the Samaritans?

"The Samaritans occupied the country formerly belonging to the tribe of Ephraim and the half-tribe of Manasseh. The capital of the country was Samaria, formerly a large and splendid city. When the ten tribes were carried away into captivity to Assyria, the King of Assyria sent people from Cutha, Ava, Hamath, and Sepharvaim to inhabit Samaria (2 Kings 17:24; Ezra 4:2-11). These foreigners intermarried with the Israelite population that was still in and around Samaria. These 'Samaritans', at first, worshiped the idols of their own nations, but, being troubled with lions, they supposed it was because they had not honored the God of that territory. A Jewish priest was therefore sent to them from Assyria, however, this priest held onto and gave false teaching. The Samaritans embraced a religion that was a mixture of Judaism and idolatry (2 Kings 17:33). Because the Israelite inhabitants of Samaria had intermarried with the foreigners and adopted their idolatrous religion, Samaritans were generally considered 'half breeds' and were universally despised by the Jews.

"Additional grounds for animosity between the Israelites and Samaritans arose after the return from Babylon, when the Jews began rebuilding the temple. While Nehemiah was engaged in building the walls of Jerusalem, the Samaritans vigorously attempted to halt the undertaking (Nehemiah 6:1-14)." [12,13]

The Lord said to me, the church has done the same thing as the Samaritans. They held onto the pagan ways. Now we must worship the Father in Spirit and in truth. Through all that the Lord taught me about Jezebel and Ashtoreth. I developed a seminar titled "Releasing a Jehu Anointing to Take Down Jezebel.

Chapter 17

Building God's House of Worship

—◦⊰☙⊱◦—

*A*s I began to teach what the Lord gave me, not everyone was accepting of it - it was not popular. When I took the coffee bar off the foundation of the ministry, I had to be obedient and speak only what the Father wanted me to speak. People left the ministry.

Around this time our lease was up in the ministry building. The owners were not going to renew it, because they wanted to tear down and rebuild. We would have to look for another building.

We began looking for a new office space. Rents were high, and landlords wanted us to sign a contract stating every year there would be a five percent increase in the rent. We could not find anything that fit our needs or that we could afford. Benjamin kept telling me he did not want to pay someone else's mortgage. He said that we should purchase our own building.

We had been out of the old building around eight months. I felt discouraged. I was back ministering in my home, and the people who were still with the ministry kept telling me we needed a building.

With the help of my daughter Pamela, who is in real estate, we found our new church building. The church was built in 1923 and is in the historical area of La Verne, California. As soon as we found this building we knew this was the one.

God pushed us through the door; we closed escrow in thirty days. While we were in escrow the Lord gave me these scriptures.

Only be strong and very courageous, that you may observe to do according to all the law which Moses My servant commanded you; do not turn from it to the right hand or to the left, that you may prosper wherever you go. This Book of the Law shall not depart from your mouth, but you shall meditate in it day and night, that you may observe to do according to all that is written in it. For then you will make your way prosperous, and then you will have good success. Have I not commanded you? Be strong and of good courage; do not be afraid, nor be dismayed, for the LORD (Yahweh) your God is with you wherever you go. (Joshua 1:7-9) (emphasis added)

...and they commanded the people, saying, "When you see the ark of the covenant of the Lord your God, and the priests, the Levites, bearing it, then you shall set out from your place and go after it (Joshua 3:3).

The Lord said the ark represents His anointing, and just as the children of Israel had to follow after the priest and the Aark, I was to follow the lead of the Holy Spirit, to be guided by His eye and not a bit in my mouth. Then He told me to teach the people to become the church/ecclesia (the calledout ones, congregation), and not to just attend church. I had never walked this way before.

And He gave some apostles: and some, prophets: and some, evangelists: and some pastors and teachers:. For the <u>PERFECTING</u> of the saints, for the work of the ministry, for the edifying of the body of Christ: Till we all come in the unity of the faith, and the knowledge of the Son of God (Elohim), unto a <u>PERFECT</u> man, unto the measure of the stature (maturity) of the fullness of Christ. Paul goes on to say that the children of God (Elohim) are not *to be tossed to and fro, and carried about with every wind of false doctrine, ... but speaking truth in love* (Ephesians 4:11-14). (emphasis added)

This is our first church plant. We have seen many miracles since we have become the ecclesia. It would take a whole other book to write down all the miracles we have seen. We have been in this building for seven years and that is a huge miracle in itself.

From that Monday morning that the Lord brought correction, I went through a spiritual tumbling. My belief system took a hard hit. The Lord reminded me of a vision. He had given to me years earlier. I was in a stream and the water was up to my ankles. Upstream I could see a dam. In this vision, the Lord said that the wall of this dam would be broken, the water was going to hit me, and when it did, I was going to tumble spiritually. Emotionally and spiritually this felt more like I was in white water rapids being turned every which way, feeling like I was going to drown, gasping for air. I would find a rock and hold on for a few minutes, until I caught my breath, just to be pulled back out for more tumbling.

So much of what I had been taught and believed was challenged. At one point I wanted to go back to what I had always believed and forget I ever learned any of this. The Lord asked me, "How are you going to go to the nations and teach others that their culture and traditions are not from Me? How do you expect them to receive the truth if you cannot let go of your false beliefs and the traditions of men that make My word of no effect?"

Chapter 18

The Feasts of the Lord

---

*T*he eight months that we were without a building, the Lord had me studying. I never studied so hard in all of my life. The Lord showed me Satan counterfeited God's holy days. I kept hearing the Holy Spirit tell me Christmas was a counterfeit. However, I kept thinking, "I know *Yeshua* was born... but when?" I sat in prayer and asked God, "When was *Yeshua* really born?" Within fifteen minutes he showed me the Feast of Tabernacles in Leviticus 23. I had never read about the Feasts and had not been taught about them. I had read about Passover in the New Testament, but when I read the word "Passover", I would read it as if it were written "Easter". That is what I was always taught.

A rich heritage was lost when the Christian church, in the second century began to sever the connection with the Jewish people and eventually stop celebrating the Feasts of the Lord (*Yahweh*). *Yeshua* said to the Samaritan woman at the well, *You worship what you do not know; we know what we worship,* (John 4:22).

After the birth, death and resurrection of *Yeshua*, the early Church fell into idolatry as the leaders led the people away from the faith of the first-century teachings of *Yeshua* and His disciples. Several hundred years later, Christianity became separated from the original Jewish Church, which believed in *Yeshua* as Messiah, kept the Sabbath, observed the Biblical Festivals and followed the Torah (first five books of the Bible). In doing so, the Christian Church began to mix the worship of God (*Elohim*) with the pagan religions around them. How did this all happen?

The first Church consisted of Jewish believers (Acts 2) and worshiped with non-believers in the synagogues. After Peter's revelation in Acts 10, approximately ten years later, the first Gentile conversions took place at Cornelius' house. However, the Gentile ways of worshiping their pagan gods were explicitly prohibited. In Acts 15:19, 20, four minimum requirements were given to the new Gentile converts. The Gentiles were also encouraged to grow in the things of the Torah and to attend synagogue every Sabbath to learn of their new faith (Acts 15:21).

Gentile believers soon began to outnumber the Jewish believers. As Paul warned, wolves within the church came to divide the new believers. After the destruction of the Temple in 70 A.D., Messianic Jews and Gentile believers became less and less welcome in the synagogues. When the Romans won the war, it was not very popular to be associated with Judaism. Prior to 100 A.D., many Gentile believers had separated themselves from the Jews, the synagogue, worshiping on the Sabbath, and celebrating the feasts.

In 325 A.D., Emperor Constantine officially declared, at the Council of Nicea (Roman decree), that worshiping on the Sabbath or in a synagogue was prohibited, as well as celebrating the Jewish feasts. In order to become a Christian under Constantine's reign, a new Jewish believer had to renounce all customs, rights, unleavened breads and feasts ...new moons... synagogues, Sabbaths... everything Jewish, every right, law and custom. To make an even more defined division of the two sects, Constantine declared that Christians would worship only on the first day of the week. The first day of the week was now called Sunday, the day of the sun god. He further changed the observance of Passover to the spring pagan holiday of Ishtar (Ashtoreth), now known as Easter. He also tied the birth of *Yeshua* to the pagan winter solstice, the birthday of Baal (Nimrod) on December 25, now known as Christmas. Nowhere in Scripture are we told to celebrate the birth of *Yeshua*, but we are commanded in Leviticus 23 to celebrate the Feast of Tabernacles. (This is when *Yeshua* was born). Thus, we began to lose our Jewish roots as pagan idolatry entered into the worship of the God (*Elohim*) of Israel.

*And the Lord spoke to Moses, saying, "Speak to the children of Israel, and say to them: **'the feasts of the Lord, which you shall pro-claim to be holy convocations**, these are My feasts"* (Leviticus 23:1-2). (emphasis added)

We are now living in times of restoration preceding the Messiah's return. Understanding the **prophetic fulfillment** of the Biblical Feasts is part of this restoration to prepare us for His coming. The way in which *Yeshua* fulfilled God's (*Elohim*) feasts is a fascinating study. God (*Elohim*) provides picture after picture of His entire plan for the salvation of mankind and one of the most startling prophetic pictures is outlined for us in God's (*Elohim*) Feasts of Leviticus 23. No wonder Satan has counterfeited them. In Genesis 3:15, God (*Elohim*) said he would crush the serpent's head through the seed of the woman. As we understand these feast days and how *Yeshua* fulfilled them, we see the plan of salvation. When the children of Israel kept these feast days it was to show the nations the plan of salvation.

Three words are used to describe the Feasts of the LORD (*Yahweh*). They are:

- *Moed* – appointments, set time, cycle, or assembly
- *Miqra* – convocation or rehearsal
- *Chag* – feast, to move in a circle, dance, celebration, rejoicing

The Feasts of the LORD (*Yahweh*) are, in other words, sacred gatherings or convocations. They are to be celebrated at appointed, set times. The people of God are to rehearse and celebrate God's (*Elohim*) salvation through the Messiah: all that He has done as well as what he will do.

All the Scriptures bear witness to *Yeshua*, Moses wrote about Him.

You search the Scriptures, for in them you think you have eternal life; and these are they which testify of Me. . . . For if you believed Moses, you would believe Me; for he wrote about Me (John 5: 39, 46).

Then He said to them, "These are the words which I spoke to you while I was still with you, that all things must be fulfilled which were written in the Law (Torah) of Moses and the Prophets and the Psalms (TaNak) concerning Me" (Luke 24:44).

All the Feasts of the Lord (*Yahweh*) have their prophetic fulfillment in Jerusalem. They are rehearsals for the great Feast in Jerusalem in the kingdom of God (*Elohim*). *I say to you that many will come from the East and the West, and sit down with Abraham, Isaac and Jacob in the kingdom of heaven* (Matthew 8:11).

132

The Hebrew word for feasts (*moadim*) literally means "appointed times." God (*Elohim*) has carefully planned and orchestrated the timing and sequence of each of these seven feasts to reveal to us a special story. The annual feasts of the LORD (*Yahweh*) are spread over seven months of the Jewish calendar, at set times appointed by God (*Elohim*). They are still celebrated by observant Jews today. For both Jews and Gentiles who have placed their faith in *Yeshua*, the Jewish Messiah, these special days demonstrate the work of redemption through God's (*Elohim*) Son.

The first of these Feasts of the LORD (*Yahweh*) is the Sabbath, I think of this day as a date day with my betrothed bridegroom, a time to renew soul, spirit and body.

Sabbath–"*Six days shall work be done, but the seventh day is a Sabbath of solemn rest, a holy convocation. You shall do no work on it; it is the Sabbath of the Lord in all your dwellings*" (Leviticus 23:3).

At the creation, *Elohim* sanctified (set apart) the Sabbath. *Then God blessed the seventh day and sanctified it, because in it He rested from all His work, which God had created and made* (Genesis 2:3). We are to imitate God's example and rest on the seventh day, as *Yahweh* rested on the seventh day of creation.

Yeshua tells us Sabbath was made for man. *Now it happened that He went through the grain fields on the Sabbath; and as they went His disciples began to pluck the heads of grain. And the Pharisees said to Him, "Look, why do they do what is not lawful on the Sabbath?" But He said to them, "Have you never read what David did when he was in need and hungry, he and those with him: how he went into the house of God in the days of Abiathar the high priest, and ate the showbread, which is not lawful to eat except for the priests, and also gave some to those who were with him?" And He said to them, "The Sabbath was made for man, and not man for the Sabbath"* (Mark 2:23-27). (emphasis added)

Also, *Come to Me, all you who labor and are heavy laden, and I will give you rest. Take My yoke upon you and learn from Me, for I am gentle and lowly in heart, and you will find rest for your souls. For My yoke is easy and My burden is light* (Matthew 11:28-30).

The Word "Sabbath" comes from the Hebrew *Shabbat*: to cease, to end, or to rest. It is the only ritual observance mentioned in the Ten Commandment and, even in modern Judaism, is considered one of the most important rituals. It is not only a day of rest, but also a day of prayer and spiritual enrichment. The Sabbath is observed every week from sundown on Friday to sundown on Saturday, and has a two-fold significance. It is both a remembrance of creation and a remembrance of the nation Israel's deliverance from the bondage of Egypt.

Observe the Sabbath day, to keep it holy, as the LORD (Yahweh) your God commanded you. Six days you shall labor and do all your work, but the seventh day is the Sabbath of the LORD (Yahweh) your God. In it you shall do no work: you, nor your son, nor your daughter, nor your male servant, nor your female servant, nor your ox, nor your donkey, nor any of your cattle, nor your stranger who is within your gates, that your male servant and your female servant may rest as well as you. **And remember that you were a slave in the land of Egypt, and the LORD (Yahweh) your God brought you out from there by a mighty hand and by an outstretched arm;** *therefore the LORD (Yahweh) your God commanded you to keep the Sabbath day* (Deuteronomy 5:12-15). (emphasis added)

Israel had been enslaved in Egypt. As a slave you had no rest. You had to work seven days a week. Now, under Sabbath rules, they were to rest themselves and allow their bondservants to rest, both of which were radical concepts in ancient times. No work was done, nor did anyone fast on the Sabbath, since it was considered a day of joy. Meals were often more elaborate and eaten more leisurely.

Prophetically we see there remains a rest; *there remains therefore a rest for the people of God* (Hebrews 4:9). Because of God's own emphasis on the Sabbath, both literally and spiritually, and since a thousand years to the LORD (*Yahweh*) is as a day (Psalm 90:4; 2 Peter 3:8), ancient and modern scholars see the seventh millennium as the Sabbath Millennium, with many prophetic implications; namely, the return of the LORD (*Yahweh*) and His 1,000-year reign on the earth.

Other examples exist of God dealing with His people's redemption where the number seven is significant. Along with Sabbath we see a seven-year cycle. Under Hebrew law the land was to rest and a servant was to serve six years and then be set free in the seventh year without paying anything.

Upon entering the Promised Land 3,500 years ago, God (*Elohim*) told the Israelites to observe a **"Year of Jubilee"** every 50 years. The Year of Jubilee was the year of restoration, proclamation of liberty and release from bondage as commanded by God in Leviticus 25:8-17: "Count seven Sabbaths of years — seven times seven years — so that the seven Sabbaths of years amount to a period of 49 years." Could it possibly be the year of the rapture is a Year of Jubilee?

The next three of the seven feasts occur during the springtime (Passover-Unleavened Bread, First Fruits, and Feast of Weeks). The final three holy days (Trumpets, The Day of Atonement, and Tabernacles) occur during the fall, all within a short fifteen-day period.

Passover (Leviticus 23:5) – Passover and the Feast of Unleavened Bread are observed in the spring. God (*Elohim*) said this was to be the New Year. The Passover is a celebration of how God took the children of Israel out of slavery. When the Israelites cried out to God, He called on Moses and Aaron to set them free.

With miracles and great power, God set the Israelites free from their hopeless situation. The angel of death passed over all of the Israelites in Egypt, because the blood of a lamb had been applied to the doorposts of their houses. *Yeshua* used this image to describe his impending death. His blood, shed on the cross, would cover the sins of his people and would save them from spiritual death. (1 Corinthians 5:7b) When we apply the blood of our Passover lamb (*Yeshua*) to the doorpost of our hearts, we too enter into the new covenant that our Father made with the house of Israel and the house of Judah. *For this is the covenant that I will make with the house of Israel after those days, says the LORD (Yahweh): I will put My laws in their mind and write them on their hearts; and I will be their God (Elohim), and they shall be My people* (Hebrews 8:10). *Yeshua* said at Passover as He took the third cup after supper, which is the cup of redemption, *...This cup is the new covenant in My blood, which is shed for you"* (Luke 22:20).

Unleavened Bread (Leviticus 23:6) – Unleavened bread represents sinlessness. God was symbolically cleansing Israel of sin for 7 days. In an observant Jewish home, there is a thorough cleaning of the home, with the goal of removing all leaven crumbs and food. They pack all their leavened food in a box and sell it to their neighbor, who keeps it for them. When the Feast of Unleavened Bread is finished, seven days later, they buy it back. The mother of the home cleans the house and boxes all the leaven. She leaves a few crumbs for the father to do the official ceremonial cleansing.

The father gathers the children and walks around the house with a candle, a feather, and a wooden spoon. He acts like he does not know where the remaining leavened crumbs are, and finally, he "finds them." He sweeps them onto the spoon with the feather and goes to the back door. He prays to God that they had cleansed the home according to His command and then drops the crumbs into a small fire he has prepared in the backyard.

What significance did it have for the children of Israel? They were taken out of bondage and sanctified, set apart as God's chosen people for His great name, so the world may know Him.

What prophetic significance does this have for us? This feast pointed to the Messiah's sinless life, making Him the perfect sacrifice for our sins. Leaven is a symbol for sin in both the Old and New Testaments. In the New Testament we read: *Your glorying is not good. Do you not know that a little leaven leavens the whole lump? Therefore purge out the old leaven, that you may be a new lump, since you truly are unleavened. For indeed Christ, our Passover, was sacrificed for us. Therefore let us keep the feast, not with old leaven, nor with the leaven of malice and wickedness, but with the unleavened bread of sincerity and truth* (1 Corinthians 5:6-8).

We are to let the Lord search our hearts for sin with the light of the Holy Spirit, just as diligently as the father searches the house for leaven. Then we need to get rid of it by repenting and turning away from it. Through this perfect sacrifice, we are sanctified. *But now having been set free from sin and having become slaves of God (Elohim), you have your fruit to holiness, and the end, everlasting life* (Romans 6:22). *...But you were washed, but you were sanctified, but you were justified in the name of the Lord Jesus (Yeshua) and by the Spirit of our God (Elohim)* (1 Corinthians 6:11). *Now may the God (Elohim) of peace himself sanctify you completely, and may your whole spirit, soul and body be kept blameless at the coming of our LORD (Yahweh) Jesus Christ (Yeshua).* (I Thessalonians 5:23).

First Fruits (Leviticus 23:9-10) *And the LORD (Yahweh) spoke to Moses, saying, "Speak to the children of Israel, and say to them: 'When you come into the land which I give to you, and reap its harvest, then you shall bring a sheaf of the first fruits of your harvest to the priest."* This pointed to the Messiah's resurrection as the first fruits of the righteous. . Paul refers to him, *But now Christ is risen from the dead, and has become the first fruits of those who have fallen asleep.For since by man came death, by Man also came the* *resurrection of the dead. For as in Adam all die, even so in Christ all shall be made alive.But each one in his own order: Christ the first fruits, afterward those who are Christ's at His coming.Then comes the end, when He delivers the kingdom to God (Elohim) the Father, when He puts an end to all rule and all authority and power.For He must reign till He has put all enemies under His feet.The last enemy that will be destroyed is death* (I Corinthians 15:20-26).

Weeks or Pentecost (Leviticus 23:16) – It commemorates the giving of the Law (Torah) at Mount Sinai, fifty days after the Children of Israel were set free from their bondage by the blood of the lamb on the door post. It occurs fifty days after the beginning of the Feast of Unleavened Bread and points to the great harvest of souls and the gift of the Holy Spirit (*Ruach Hakodesh*) for both Jew and Gentile, who are brought into the Kingdom of God (*Elohim*) (see Acts 2). The Church was established on this day when God (*Elohim*) poured out His Holy Spirit (*Ruach Hakodesh*) and 3,000 Jews responded to Peter's great sermon and his first proclamation of the Gospel.

For I will take you from among the nations, gather you out of all countries, and bring you into your own land. Then I will sprinkle clean water on you, and you shall be clean; I will cleanse you from all your filthiness and from all your idols. I will give you a new heart and put a new spirit within you; I will take the heart of stone out of your flesh and give you a heart of flesh. I will put My Spirit within you and cause you to walk in My statutes, and you will keep My judgments and do them (Ezekiel 36:24-27).

Through Passover-Unleavened and Pentecost we see this scripture fulfilled. The children of Israel, like us, could not keep the loving instructions that God (*Elohim*) gave them on Mount Sinai. There was nothing wrong with God's (*Elohim*) Torah (Loving instructions). But there was something wrong with men's hearts. Through *Yeshua's* blood we can enter into this covenant with our Father and He will take out our stony hearts, give us a heart of flesh, write His precepts on it, then put His spirit in us, so we can walk in His statutes. We further read, *Then you shall dwell in the land that I gave to your fathers; you shall be My people, and I will be your God* (Elohim) (Ezekiel 36:28).

Feast of Trumpets (Leviticus 23:24) *Speak unto the children of Israel, saying, in the seventh month, in the first day of the month,* *shall ye have a Sabbath, a memorial of blowing of trumpets, an holy convocation* (Leviticus 23:24). The Feast of the Trumpets begins on Rosh Hashanah, the first day of the seventh month, Tishri. It is also considered the Jewish New Year. The ancient rabbis believed that God began Creation on the first day of the seventh month, which is Tishri. (**However, when Israel came out of bondage from Egypt, God told them Passover was to be the New Year.**) The sounding of the trumpet was used to call His people to repentance, to awake from sin, because ten days later, the holiest day, the Day of Atonement (Yom Kippur) would occur.

This trumpet is called a "shofar." It is made from a ram's horn, in remembrance of the ram that God had provided when Abraham offered Isaac as a sacrifice to the LORD (*Yahweh*). God provided the ram instead of Isaac. Thus, Abraham named the place *Yahweh*-**yireh** "God will provide" or "God is our provider."

Many believe this day points to the rapture of the Church when *Yeshua* will appear in the heavens as He comes for us, His bride. The Rapture is always associated in Scripture with the blowing of a loud trumpet (shofar).

But I do not want you to be ignorant, brethren, concerning those who have fallen asleep, lest you sorrow as others who have no hope. For if we believe that Jesus (Yeshua) died and rose again, even so God (Elohim) will bring with Him those who sleep in Jesus (Yeshua). For this we say to you by the word of the LORD (Yahweh), that we who are alive and remain until the coming of the LORD (Yahweh) will by no means precede those who are asleep. For the LORD (Yahweh) Himself will descend from heaven with a shout, with the voice of an archangel, and with the trumpet (Shofar) of God (Elohim). And the dead in Christ will rise first. Then we who are alive and remain shall be caught up together with them in the clouds to meet the LORD (Yahweh) in the air. And thus we shall always be with the LORD (Yahweh). Therefore comfort one another with these words (1 Thessalonians 4:13-18).

In a moment, in the twinkling of an eye, at the last trumpet: or the trumpet (Shofar) will sound, and the dead will be raised incorruptible, and we shall be changed (I Corinthians 15:52).

Day of Atonement (Lev. 23:26-32) The holiest day in the Jewish year (a fast day not a feast day), is the Day of Atonement (Yom Kippur). It is spent in fasting, prayer, and confession. On this particular day, each year, God (*Elohim*) gave grace to every individual, so they would be forgiven.

When the temple still existed in Jerusalem, once a year the high priest would sacrifice a bull and a goat. Then with the goats blood the High Priest would enter the Holy of Holies behind the veil in the temple, where the Shekinah glory was to make atonement for the nation when the blood was sprinkled on the mercy seat.

Yeshua has provided our atonement: *But Christ came as High Priest of the good things to come, with the greater and more perfect tabernacle not made with hands, that is, not of this creation. Not with the blood of goats and calves, but with His own blood He entered the Most Holy Place once for all, having obtained eternal redemption. For if the blood of bulls and goats and the ashes of a heifer, sprinkling the unclean, sanctifies for the purifying of the flesh, how much more shall the blood of Christ, who through the eternal Spirit offered Himself without spot to God, cleanse your conscience from dead works to serve the living God* (Hebrews 9:11-14).

This is also the day Israel believes that your names either remain in the Book of Life or they are blotted out. We see Moses pleaded with God atop Mount Horeb, after the children of Israel committed the great sin of the golden calf. He cried, *...Oh, these people have committed a great sin, and have made for themselves a god of gold! Yet now, if Thou will, forgive their sin—but if not, blot me out from Your book which You hast written!* (Exodus 32:31-32).

And who would be blotted out of the book? God's response to Moses' plea for the children of Israel was: and the Lord said to Moses, "Whoever has sinned against Me, I will blot him out of My book." (Exodus 32:33).

Praise God! If we have received *Yeshua* as our Lord (*Yahweh*) and Savior, then our names are written in the Lamb's Book of Life! As we see in Revelation, *So they worshiped the dragon who gave authority to the beast; and they worshiped the beast, saying, "Who is like the beast? Who is able to make war with him?" And he was given a mouth speaking great things and blasphemies, and he was given authority to continue for forty-two months. Then he opened his mouth in blasphemy against God, to blaspheme His name, His tabernacle, and those who dwell in heaven. It was granted to him to make war with the saints and to overcome them. And authority was given him over every tribe, tongue, and nation. All who dwell on the earth will worship him, whose names have not been written in the Book of Life of the Lamb, slain from the foundation of the world* (Revelation 13:4-8).

Tabernacles or Booths (Leviticus 23:34) – The Feast of Tabernacles is a seven-day Feast, (Exodus 23:16; 34:22; Leviticus 23:33-36, 39-43; Numbers 29:12-34; Deuteronomy 16:13-15). *Also in the fifteenth day of the seventh month, when ye have gathered in the fruit of the land, ye shall keep a feast unto the LORD (Yahweh) seven days: on the first day shall be a Sabbath, and on the eighth day shall be a Sabbath. And ye shall take you on the first day the boughs of goodly trees, branches of palm trees, and the boughs of thick trees, and willows of the brook: and ye shall rejoice before the LORD (Yahweh) your God seven days. And ye shall keep it a feast unto the LORD (Yahweh) seven days in the year. ye shall celebrate it in the seventh month. Ye shall dwell in booths seven days; all that are Israelites born shall dwell in booths: That your generations may know that I made the children of Israel to dwell in booths, when I brought them out of the land of Egypt: I am the LORD (Yahweh) your God (Elohim).* (Leviticus 23:39-43)

The children of Israel were taken out of Egypt to the land that God (*Elohim*) had promised to Abram. This trip should have taken eleven days. It ended up taking forty years. However, God (*Elohim*) did not leave them nor forsake them in their wilderness time. God (Elohim) had Moses build a tabernacle, and He dwelt among them. This feast is to be kept forever to remind Israel that God tabernacled with them.

God (*Elohim*) sent *Yeshua* to tabernacle (dwell) among us in the flesh. *"And the Word became flesh, and did tabernacle among us, and we beheld his glory, glory as of an only begotten of a father, full of grace and truth." (John 1:14(YLT)*

I, along with many scholars, believe that the Feast of Tabernacles is the birth date of *Yeshua*. *Yeshua* said he would send the comforter, which is the Holy Spirit (*Ruach Hakodesh*), to dwell (tabernacle) in us until He returns.

We are the temple of God (1 Corinthians 6:19). The Bible says we are not left orphans. *Yeshua* set the example for all mankind by observing the feast himself. *On the last day, that great day of the feast,* Yeshua *stood and cried out, saying, "If anyone thirsts, let him come to Me and drink"* (John 7:37).

Further, we are told that all people in the Millennium will observe the Feast of Tabernacles, *And it shall come to pass that everyone who is left of all the nations which came against Jerusalem shall go up from year to year to worship the King, the LORD (Yahweh) of hosts, and to keep the Feast of Tabernacles. And it shall be that whichever of the families of the earth do not come up to Jerusalem to worship the King, the LORD (Yahweh) of hosts, on them there will be no rain. If the family of Egypt will not come up and enter in, they shall have no rain; they shall receive the plague with which the LORD (Yahweh) strikes the nations who do not come up to keep the Feast of Tabernacles. This shall be the punishment of Egypt and the punishment of all the nations that do not come up to keep the Feast of Tabernacles* (Zechariah 14:16-19).

As Christians, when we celebrate the LORD's (*Yahweh*) holy feast days, we put *Yeshua* in the center of the celebration as the One who came to fulfill the prophetic significance of each of them.

When we understand the significance of these days, we can understand what King David meant when he said, *He restores my soul; He leads me in the paths of righteousness for His name's sake.* (Psalm 23:3). The word *paths* is actually taken from the Hebrew root *agol,* which means to be round or a cycle. Actually, in this Psalm, David is using a phrase familiar to the Hebrew people. He is saying the Lord (*Yahweh*) leads us or guides us in the *cycles of righteousness.* The cycles of righteousness refers to the weekly and yearly return of the Feasts of the Lord (*Yahweh*). This is why the closely related word *chag* or festival, is referred to as "making a cycle." The *chaggim* are the cyclical holy days, in which the righteousness of the God (*Elohim*) of Israel is taught. It is these cycles that David is referring to. Certainly, it is beneficial to celebrate these days, if it leads one to a greater understanding and appreciation for *Yeshua's* birth, death and resurrection and the future promise of His coming.

Final Word

His Bride Without Spot or Wrinkle

—⋅⋯⋙❦⋘⋯⋅—

*Y*eshua is coming back for His bride without spot or wrinkle or any such thing. He is washing us, His bride, by His word, to present us to Himself without spot or wrinkle. *That He might sanctify and cleanse her with the washing of water by the word, that He might present her to Himself a glorious church, not having spot or wrinkle or any such thing, but that she should be holy and without blemish* (Ephesians 5:26-27).

The darkness is covering the whole earth and deep darkness is covering the people. However, the bride of Christ is making herself ready. She is becoming that glorious bride without spot or wrinkle or any such thing ready for her betrothed bridegroom as she says, Come *Yeshua*, Come!

Arise, shine; for your light has come! And the glory of the LORD (Yahweh) is risen upon you. For behold, the darkness shall cover the earth, and deep darkness the people; But the LORD (Yahweh) will arise over you, and His glory will be seen upon you (Isaiah 60:1-2).

Yeshua Testifies to the Churches

And behold, I am coming quickly, and My reward is with Me, to give to every one according to his work. I am the Alpha and the Omega, the Beginning and the End, the First and the Last." Blessed are those who do His commandments that they may have the right to the tree of life, and may enter through the gates into the city. But outside

142

*are dogs and sorcerers and sexually immoral and murderers and idolaters, and whoever loves and practices a lie. "I, Jesus (Yeshua), have sent My angel to testify to you these things in the churches. I am the Root and the Offspring of David, the Bright and Morning Star." **And the Spirit and the bride say, "Come!" And let him who hears say, "Come!"** And let him who thirsts come. Whoever desires, let him take the water of life freely." For I testify to everyone who hears the words of the prophecy of this book: If anyone adds to these things, God (Elohim) will add to him the plagues that are written in this book; and if anyone takes away from the words of the book of this prophecy, God (Elohim) shall take away his part from the Book of Life, from the holy city, and from the things which are written in this book. He who testifies to these things says, "Surely I am coming quickly." Amen. Even so, come, LORD (Yahweh) Jesus (Yeshua)! The grace of our LORD (Yahweh) Jesus (Yeshua Ha mashiah) be with you all, Amen* (Revelation 22:12-21). (emphasis added)

Shalom!

About the Author

—⚜—

$\mathcal{D}$r. Patricia has an inspiring testimony of how the Lord healed and delivered her. She was raised in a dysfunctional alcoholic home, with verbal and sexual abuse, resulting in her becoming a young mother at the age of thirteen. She has been married to Reverend Benjamin for thirty years, and has four children, six grandchildren and four great-grandchildren, two stepdaughters and four step-grandchildren.

She and her husband Reverend Benjamin Venegas founded **Without Spot or Wrinkle Ministries International in 1998.** In November of 2007, they launched their first church plant in La Verne, California. She is Senior Pastor and CEO. The congregation of Without Spot or Wrinkle Ministries International is Judeo-Christian, founded and grounded on scripture and the Word of God. They have a global mandate to restore the Bride of Christ (the Church), preparing her to be without spot or wrinkle or any such thing, for the soon return of her bridegroom, Yeshua (Ephesians 5:26). Dr. Patricia walks in an end-time restoration anointing, ministering in the power of the Holy Spirit with signs and wonders, bringing healing and restoration to the body of Christ. She is also an Author, Artist and International Speaker.

Dr. Patricia has developed a series of seminars and conferences, which she teaches in order to further accomplish this mandate.

- Spiritual Boot Camp Basic Training DVD-CDs
- Advanced Training DVD-CDs
- Strategies of the Enemy
- Boot Camp for Marriage DVD-CDs
- He Restores My Soul
- Releasing a Jehu Anointing to Take Down Jezebel

- Inner Healing and Deliverance

She also operates in the Holy Spirit gifting of counseling, described in Isaiah 61.

She has received her Doctor of Divinity Degree, Masters in Biblical Studies with emphasis on Christian Counseling and her Bachelor Degree of Theology from Promise Christian University in Pasadena, California.

She is on staff with Promise Christian University as an Professor of Counseling and Hebraic Roots.

To book Dr. Patricia for a speaking engagement at your church services, seminar/conference, retreats or other special events or to order the Boot Camp Series you can contact her office at the number below.

Without Spot or Wrinkle Ministries International
2211 3rd Street, La Verne, CA 91750
Phone: 909.593.2607
www.wosow.org

Endnotes

─ ⚬❧⚭⚬ ─

[1] http://www.trustingodamerica.com/Bride.htm

[2] http://messianicgentiles.blogspot.com/2009/06/feast-of-trumpets-yom-truah-jewish.htmJEWISH WEDDING TRADITIONS

[3] http://en.wikipedia org/wiki/The_Exorcist_(film)

[4] http://sparethekids.com/2011/10/why-foster-kids-and-adoptees-rescue-others-but-fail-at-intimacy/

[5] http://www.livescience.com/32289-how-do-oysters-make-pearls.html

[6] http://justbetweenus.org/pages/page.asp?page_id=90757

[7] http://christianity.about.com/od/biblestorysummaries/p/prod-igalson.htm

[8] http://ministeringdeliverance.com/generational_curses.php

[9] http://jimbomkamp.com/2Samuel/2Sam6p1.htm

[10] *http://www3.telus.net/trbrooks/spiritualauthority.pdf²*

[11] http://iiocc.org/associatedegreechristiancounselingcourses2.html

[12] http://www.biblelneministries.org/articles/basearch.php3?action=full&mainkey=BABYLONIAN+RELIGION+(By+Harry+A.+Ironside)

[13] http://www.ldolphin.org/semir.html

[14] *Paganism in Christmas* Part 2, by Roy A. Reinhold

[15] http://www.gotquestions.org/Samaritans.html

[16] http://www.gotquestions.org/Samaritans.html#ixzz3IsyGgr69